RECIPES

What You've Been Missing

Stuart Mizuta

Published by Stuart Mizuta
Evanston, Illinois

ISBN
Library of Congress Catalog Card Number
978-0-692-31001-4

*This book is dedicated to my parents
for all of their support
that turned an idea for a book
into reality.*

CONTENTS

Preface • X
Acknowledgements • XII
Introduction • XIII

CHAPTER 1
Recipe Development
More Than Ingredients and Techniques • 1
Consumer and Professional Recipes • 2
Ingredient Ratios • 7
Baker's Percentages in Bread Making • 13
Changing Recipe Yields • 15
Determining Nutrient Food Values •20
What You've Been Missing in Recipe Development • 23

CHAPTER 2
Reading Recipes
Interpreting Recipe Directions • 27
Cooking Methods and Techniques • 28
Identifying Recipe Methods and Techniques • 33
Professionalizing Consumer Recipes • 40
What You've Been Missing in Reading Recipes • 45

CHAPTER 3
Flavor Relationships
More Than Just Taste • 49
Experiencing Flavor in Foods • 50
Adjusting Flavor Outcomes • 55
Flavor Layering in Recipes • 59
Ingredient Pairing • 66
Preserving Natural Flavors • 68
What You've Been Missing in Flavor Relationships • 75

CHAPTER 4
Recipe Design
Translating Ideas into Reality • 81
The Design Process • 82
The Recipe Design Process • 83
Recipe Research and Concept Development • 84
Recipe Conversion • 92
Recipe Design and Development • 93
Recipe Layout • 98
What You've Been Missing by Not Designing Recipes • 109

CHAPTER 5
Evaluation
Informing Future Recipe Decisions • 113
Integrating Multiple Needs • 115
Evaluating the Process • 116
Evaluating Recipe Outcomes • 117
What You've Been Missing in Recipe Evaluation • 119

CHAPTER 6
Summary • 123
A Framework for Recipe Interpretation

APPENDIX I
Weights of Common Produce • 129

APPENDIX II
Table of Flavor Relationships • 139

APPENDIX III
Table of Ingredients by Taste Profile • 143

REFERENCES • 157

INDEX • 165

Preface

The world does not need another cookbook full of recipes. There are libraries full of great books that touch upon just about every cuisine out there. A typical Google search on the Internet yields even more recipe choices that at times can be staggering. Cooking has become so popular that the Food Network "has programming in more than 150 countries, including 24-hour networks in Great Britain, India, Asia, and Africa" (Food Network, 2014) and includes cable, website, and magazine outlets.

But access to cooking information does not guarantee that every subject has been covered at length or that presented materials are fully understood. Recipes, for the most part, are simply viewed as instruction sets, made up of ingredients and the directions on their preparation. As a set of directives, recipes issue orders on what to do and when to do it. Following these commands, there is an underlying assumption that everything will come out as planned.

In reality, recipe results can squarely hit the mark or be far afield of what was expected. People are left to figure out what happened and sometimes blame themselves, thinking they did something wrong. There must be a way to foresee problems before they appear in recipe preparation or show up in the final product.

This book offers a proactive perspective that seeks to identify potential problems before a recipe is selected for preparation and cooking. Recipe fundamentals provide a foundation for recipe interpretation that identifies what is missing in recipes people use every day. This exploration is likely different from anything you have read before. This work results from the development of recipes from an array of sources and in some cases were well written, but in many others were incomplete or incorrectly described. Personal triumph and failure have fed this book's development, as well as experiencing firsthand how professional chefs approach recipe selection.

I wrote this book to save you the time of searching through an array of culinary resources that only cover one aspect of recipe analysis and interpretation. Integrated into one source, the book will demonstrate what likely has been missing in the recipes used every day.

The approach to recipes advocated in this book results from the integration of several academic degrees as well as a diverse range of experience. These include a culinary arts degree and Culinarian Certification by the American Culinary Federation. Undergraduate and masters degrees in landscape architecture inform the problem solving approach used to analyze and develop integrated recipes. The discussion of natural flavors is an outgrowth of work that preserved vanishing native habitats in the urban environment. There is not only a need to manage for threatened and endangered species, but also for food species that hold the key to our vanishing natural flavors from the past. Since the author is committed to a life that challenges the norm, this book is intended to be different from the rest.

Acknowledgements

I was blessed to have the help and encouragement of many friends and colleagues who contributed their time, encouragement, and knowledge to this work. My sincere thanks go to Scott Byron, who has supported my career evolution for close to thirty years. His encouragement to act on my passion for cooking and the environment led me to write this book. His input during the book's development provided a business perspective from a person whose company continues to be a leading force for excellence in the field of landscape architecture.

My deepest gratitude and appreciation go to Chef Timothy Bucci CEC, CCE, CHE, who strongly encouraged me to write this book. His review made this work more useful and accessible to the reader. A very special thanks to Dr. Brian Anderson, whose scientific and ecological review strengthened the integrity and continuity of the material presented. I would also like to thank Jim Steffen, who took the time to locate and identify many of the plants talked about and photographed in this book. Thanks also to Barbara Kois, my editor and to Julie Chen who helped to refine the book layout. A special thanks also goes to Joan Begitschke who advised on the cover, text copy and layout.

A heartfelt thanks to my parents, without whose encouragement, love, and support through the years, this book would not have been possible. Finally, thanks to God, who carved out this part of my life to put forth a book that by my own hands I could never accomplish.

Introduction

Creating recipes from scratch is a process that takes time, cooking experience, and the confidence to achieve the desired result. Fortunately, there exist many recipe choices on the Internet, television, and in books and magazines. Finding a recipe can be as easy as accessing a cooking website and making a selection that has a four star rating. Too much choice may complicate the selection process but can be resolved by reviewing each version and asking the following questions:

1. Is the recipe clear on what has to be done?
2. What skill level is required to make this recipe?
3. How much time does the recipe take to prepare and cook?
4. Does the recipe contain hard-to-find or expensive ingredients?
5. Does the recipe require the use of tools or equipment not currently owned?
6. Are there any photos that show the final result?
7. Does the recipe make the right quantity of food?

These questions evaluate recipe clarity, complexity, timing, convenience, visual appearance, and quantity outcome. These considerations address the key concerns of most people but are based on the assumption that recipes provide all the information necessary to make an informed decision. Recipes generally contain a list of ingredients and a paragraph of cooking directions. Outside of this commonly accepted layout, pretty much anything goes - from detailed personal observations to almost no description at all.

What is missing in recipes is not always the same thing. This inconsistency has many probable causes, including limited page or column space or incorrect assumptions about the reader's knowledge and skill. Some recipe authors may not know what to write or just choose to write less and let the readers figure things out for themselves. Selecting a recipe is often a matter of guesswork and a little bit of luck. The reputation of the source may be the only form of guidance available. Without access to the recipe author, people are pretty much on their own.

For people who just want to cook and be done with it, there are plenty of other recipe books available. This book is for those who take an active interest in what they are cooking and passionately want to explore the inner workings of recipes. Recipe selection and interpretation take an investment of time, some sleuthing, risk taking, and sense of adventure. This effort is rewarded in recipe choices that better meet individual needs and expectations. At first the process is slow, but becomes quicker and easier as recipe patterns emerge that lead to informed decisions to stay away or to go for it. Recipes do not require knowledge of calculus, but basic math skills are necessary to determine quantities and change yields. The use of mathematics takes the guesswork out of recipe interpretation and provides sound data on which to make decisions.

There are five chapters in this book that deal with recipe basics, interpretation, flavor development, design, and evaluation. The final chapter provides a framework for recipe examination and development. Unlike many recipe books where each recipe is different, here the same recipe is broken down into its component parts to expose its structure and developmental approach. This critical analysis is what is missing from most recipe books. Recipe examples build on each other to illustrate subtle differences. Ingredient use may be the same across several recipes, but their quantities different or are measured in cups in one and by weight in another.

This is not a cookbook of recipes; those can be found elsewhere. Photographs are used to provide examples and in some cases, to describe what words cannot. Sources of information are provided along the way to help you find additional information. The end of each chapter includes a list of key points for those short on time or who want to refresh their memory. The appendices provide common weights of many ingredients used in developing recipes, a table of flavor relationships, and tables of ingredients by their taste profile.

My hope is that you will be intrigued by what you read and will be able to use what you have learned on your food journey. So let us get started. On to Chapter 1!

Chapter One

Recipe Development
More Than Ingredients and Techniques

Recipes are often discussed in the context of their ingredients and techniques, since they provide direction on cooking. Often missing from these discussions are the underlying principles that inform the selection of ingredients and choice of techniques.

These considerations were likely part of the development process but are not discussed in the published recipe people see every day. Unveiling this process gives us a glimpse into the mind of the chef, a place where some do not want to venture. Too much time spent there takes away from the act of cooking. Exploring just a little bit of the chef's world, however, fills in some blanks that help people select and develop better outcomes.

Chefs group food into broad categories that reflect their preparation method. These basic categories are useful in the discussion of recipes since they speak to the essence of a recipe's intent. *Hot foods* are prepared using a heat source such as a flame. Grilled Mahi Mahi is one example.

Cold foods are prepared in a cold kitchen, historically a storage area or pantry. Food examples include salads, cold appetizers, smoked foods, and sausages, among others. *Garde manger* (gahr mohn-azhj) is the French word that historically identified the kitchen location where these foods were stored. In today's professional kitchen it refers to the area where these foods are made, the people who work there and an area of specialization in culinary arts.

Baking and pastries refers to foods that are baked in an oven or are prepared as pastries. Bread, pies, and tarts are good examples. These simple food categories are a place to start before getting into all the recipe detail.

Recipes are not all intended for consumer use. This actuality may surprise those who buy books to get restaurant recipes. Chefs who write for the home cook have to consider their audience just like other professionals who develop products for those outside their profession.

There are actually two types of recipes, those for consumers and those for cooking professionals. Understanding their differences may lead to different recipe selections and better outcomes if aspects of both can be combined. The ingredients list is something we scrutinize to make sure the foods we enjoy are included. Chefs also develop recipes with ingredients in mind, but they also consider the mathematical relationships between them that are important to the recipe's success. An individual ingredient quantity is important, but its relationship to other ingredient amounts also matters.

These ratios are important to understand since they form the basis of many recipes. Acknowledging their presence and using them to uncover recipe errors can lead to better cooking decisions.

Along the same lines, recipe yield and portion size, when provided, are exceedingly helpful in changing recipe outputs. Inevitably, recipes do not make enough or make too much food to meet the current need. Understanding how to use recipe yield and portion size to change recipe yields is highly valuable in meeting the needs of larger parties or buffet situations. Chefs deal with yield adjustments on a regular basis.

People sometimes assume that making a recipe from scratch is better for you than eating its processed counterpart. Calculating nutrient values for the ingredients in recipes is a way to definitively know the recipe made has the nutritional content expected. The tools to perform this analysis work are discussed at the end of this chapter. You may be surprised by the nutrient content of everyday foods.

Consumer and Professional Recipes

When watching television shows and reading popular books and magazines, recipes used by consumers and culinary professionals appear to be the same.

Seeing a chef on television make one of their recipes suggests its ingredients and techniques are the same as those used in their restaurants. This is not always the case since what is showcased has been likely tailored for the consumer. Ingredients may be substituted for those available in grocery stores and techniques simplified to reflect the assumed skill of the average home cook.

Part of the appeal of chef recipes is that they follow popular conventions, making them widely accessible. People do not have to think twice about reading and understanding a recipe from a popular book or one written by a professional chef. These consumer recipes written by culinary professionals typically contain an ingredient list followed by a set of directions to prepare the product. Dry ingredient quantities are measured in cups and spoons and liquids in fluid ounces. The yield or quantity produced is typically small and designed for a family or small gathering. Directions are written for people with limited or no culinary training.

Consumer recipes are designed to be easy to follow, generally cook in a short amount of time, and do not take long to prepare. These time savings, however, may be the result of eliminating or combining steps. The use of prepared ingredients, such as canned broths, eliminates the hours of time required to make a stock beforehand. In either case, prepared store bought ingredients have been made ahead of time and are ready to use before the television demonstration starts.

Consumer recipes are numerous on the Internet and are the first choice for people to use because search engines make finding a recipe as easy as a mere click of a button. Websites like Epicurious.com are one-stop-shop experiences that have recipes, a message board and articles pertaining to food preparation, restaurant dining, entertaining, and even kitchen equipment.

Popular television shows like "America's Test Kitchen" have their own web presence and make their recipes available. Professional chef websites provide recipe details from their television shows and promote their restaurants and cookware. Food manufacturers also have websites. Nasoya, the manufacturer of organic tofu, has a range of different recipes on their site.

Recipe websites focused on a particular category of cooking are also available. One such site, TheFreshLoaf.com, is a place where amateur artisan bakers can post comments or recipes or create baker blogs.

Outside of the digital world, consumer recipes can be found in libraries that contain books, magazines, and journals. Sometimes forgotten are fundraising cookbooks that contain recipes from church members or other non-profit organizations. The manner in which these recipes are written can be challenging to understand at times, but these cookbooks also offer interesting perspectives on those who publish them.

The term professional recipe sounds intimidating, especially when restaurant chefs write books that contain consumer versions of their restaurant recipes. Professional recipes are not necessarily intimidating but are written for a different audience and meet different needs from consumer versions.

Chefs and cooks have formal culinary training, experience, or both. The home cook may have some cooking experience or know nothing at all about cooking. Professional recipes meet the needs of dozens, hundreds, or thousands of people. Consumer recipes fulfill the need of a single person, family, or small group. These differences result in professional recipes that are characterized by their consistency and consumer recipes that differ, depending on their maker.

In a restaurant situation, product consistency is very important so that each person gets the same food experience every time. Consistency is why people come back, knowing the great dish they had this week will be great next week as well. Without recipe consistency, food costs would be difficult to calculate, affecting restaurant profitability. The need for consistency in professional kitchens leads to the development of standardized recipes that produce a known quality and quantity of food for a specific kitchen situation.

These types of recipes are not found in cookbooks. Manufacturers do not provide them. Standardized recipes work because they take into account the specific conditions of an operation. They specify the amount and type of each ingredient, the methods, yield and serving size for a particular recipe (Labensky & Hause, 2007). Standardized recipes are not the ones that people see in popular cookbooks found on store shelves or the ones demonstrated on television.

The overall layout of professional and consumer recipes may look the same, but the information provided varies. In some cases, the method of preparation in professional recipes is not explained in detail. This may appear to be a major omission and run counter to the idea of consistency, but when the method is a known standard to culinary professionals, providing directions is redundant.

A basic French vinaigrette salad dressing is made up of four ingredients. The vinegar, salt, and pepper are mixed first and the oil is added last. This procedure is always the same. A trained or experience cook does not need this information written down for a basic vinaigrette recipe, just the quantities and ingredient types. Do not be suprised if a professional recipe has no directions.

But professional recipes do provide essential information that allows them to be scaled up or down to meet changing needs and help control food costs. Ingredients are measured mostly by their weight and not their volume, which is the amount of space they take up in a container such as a measuring cup. An ingredient's weight refers to its heaviness as measured on a scale. The units of measure can be expressed in ounces, pounds, or grams, depending on the amount of the ingredient. One pound of water sounds strange at first, but is an easier unit of measure to deal with if all the other ingredients are weighed as well. Measuring ingredients by their weight eliminates the use of cup and spoon measures, simplifying the measuring process.

Since many ingredients are bought in bulk, measuring by weight fits within that purchasing strategy. Professional recipes also indicate the number of servings and the serving size of the recipe. Knowing how many servings a recipe makes helps in meal planning. The size of a serving can be used to calculate food costs and nutritional values, and is useful when scaling up a recipe to a larger quantity. Some consumer recipes provide the number of recipe servings, but typically not the serving size.

Traditional vinaigrettes illustrate the differences between consumer and professional recipes. The consumer version of Basic French Dressing (Recipe 1-1) contains a title, but no yield information that indicates the amount produced. The number of servings and the serving size are also omitted. As expected, ingredients are quantified in cup and spoon measures. Adding up the quantities of vinegar and canola oil, the recipe makes one cup of dressing. Directions tell the user how to prepare the vinaigrette and advise on its storage and service.

The professional recipe for the same Basic French Dressing (Recipe 1-2) contains the same title but provides the recipe yield, the number of servings, and the serving size. The larger yield of one quart is enough for a large group of people. The vinegar and oil are expressed in fluid ounces since they are liquids and ounces quantify the amount of salt and pepper. The type of vinegar and oil is not specified since that will be determined by the pairing of the dressing with salad components.

The dressing preparation is shown as a series of steps in numerical order

---

Recipe 1-1

Basic French Dressing

¼ C	red wine vinegar
¾ C	canola oil
½ tsp.	salt
¼ tsp.	pepper

Directions

In a small bowl, combine the vinegar, salt and pepper and mix well. Whisk in the oil gradually until the ingredients emulsify together. Allow the dressing to rest in the refrigerator for a few hours so that the flavors can blend. Whisk again immediately before use.

Recipe 1-2

Basic French Dressing (Yield 1 Qt., 32 servings, 1 oz. each)

8 fl. oz.	vinegar
24 fl. oz.	oil
.44 oz.	salt
.06 oz.	pepper

Method

1. Choose an oil and vinegar combination that will complement the food.
2. Combine the vinegar, salt and pepper and mix well in a bowl.
3. Whisk in the oil gradually until the ingredients emulsify together.
4. Rest in the cooler for 15 minutes and then taste with a salad component. Make adjustments in seasonings as necessary. Cover and hold in the cooler until service.

---

and the word "method" replaces "directions". Although the preparation of the dressing is the same in both recipes, the taste of the salad dressing is tested and adjusted with the salt and pepper (seasonings) if necessary. Culinary professionals evaluate the taste of their food as ingredients can vary a bit from batch to batch. These fine adjustments are one of the things that produce better recipe outcomes.

Professional recipes are therefore written for people with a greater level of culinary knowledge. Recipe ingredients are often quantified by weight instead of in cup and spoon measures. Serving and portion size are provided so the recipe outcome can be adjusted to meet the anticipated need.

Ingredient Ratios

Recipe ingredients and their quantities typically take the form of a list to facilitate quick review of recipe contents. Listed separately, ingredients appear to function independently. Home cooks often focus on the type of ingredients, especially where to buy them or whether they are on hand.

Being comfortable with what goes into a recipe is important, but it is not the only consideration. Known as ratios, ingredient quantities form comparative relationships that are important to a recipe's outcome and development. Traditional salad dressings provide good examples of ingredient ratios

The professional recipe for Basic French dressing (Recipe 1-2) is one such example. Based on ingredient weight instead of volume measures, ratios are easier to identify. Integer-based quantities are mathematically easier to work with than fractional cup measures used in consumer recipes. Looking at the recipe's liquids, there is a three-to-one ratio between the oil (24 oz.) and vinegar (8 oz.). Knowing this relationship is integral to the recipe's development and is useful when making more or less of the product. Doubling the amount of oil to 48 ounces requires 16 ounces of vinegar to maintain the same three-to-one ratio between the ingredients. Reducing the recipe yield in half requires 12 ounces of oil to 4 ounces of vinegar.

The ratio between ingredients can also provide insight into a recipe's flavor outcome. Oil in an amount that is three times greater than the vinegar in a salad dressing points to its important role in flavor development. Traditionally, the oil used in basic vinaigrette dressing is neutral-tasting to allow the flavor of the vinegar to come through. Canola oil is a good example. Some people nevertheless prefer the taste of extra-virgin olive oil because of its strong flavor.

Bread dipped in extra virgin olive oil highlights the flavor of the oil, not the bread. Using extra virgin olive oil in a salad dressing can shift its flavor to the taste of the oil and not the vinegar. This could be desirable to some people, but it greatly alters the flavor intent of the original recipe. The flavor of olive oil can be introduced into a salad dressing by keeping the overall ratio between the oil and vinegar the same by blending olive oil (not extra virgin) in a 1:1 ratio with canola oil (Recipe 1-3). This way the olive oil flavor comes through but does not mask the flavor of the vinegar. Ratios used in this manner can change flavor outcomes but also maintain the integrity of the original recipe. Adjusting the recipe yield later, as the need arises, is also easier using ratios as a guide.

Recipe 1-3

Basic French Dressing – Revised (Yield 1 Qt., 32 servings, 1 oz. each)

8 fl. oz.	vinegar
12 fl. oz.	olive oil
12 fl. oz.	canola oil
.44 oz.	salt
.06 oz.	pepper

Method

1. Choose an oil and vinegar combination that will complement the food.
2. Combine the vinegar, salt and pepper and mix well in a bowl.
3. Whisk in the oil gradually until the ingredients emulsify together.
4. Rest in the cooler for 15 minutes and then taste with a salad component. Make adjustments in seasonings as necessary. Cover and hold in the cooler until service.

White stocks are also good examples of ratio-driven recipes. Stocks are flavored liquids used in the production of many foods, including soups, sauces, and braises. White stocks are primarily made from veal, chicken, or beef bones and cold water. The bones in white stock are not browned in an oven before use, hence the name white stock.

Cold water is very important to stock development. Starting with cold water allows the bone impurities, commonly referred to as scum, to coagulate and rise to the surface where they are removed with the use of a ladle. Starting with hot water has the opposite effect. Impurities coalesce more quickly in hot water, remain dispersed in the stock, and do not rise to the surface. Remaining suspended in the liquid, the stock becomes clouded (Ruhlman, 2009).

Some may not care if their stock is cloudy, but a clear stock makes a difference in the preparation of professionally made dishes. Only bones are used in the development of white stock. The use of meat and bones turns a stock into a broth. Broths are finished products that can be used alone and sometimes contain salt. In a home situation, stocks and broths are probably interchangeable. When using commercially produced broth instead of stock, check its salt content. In some cases, adjustments may have to be made to the sodium content of a recipe.

The ratio of bones to water in white stock can vary widely. A ratio one-to-one (1:1) bones to water will yield a strongly flavored stock that is very gelatinous (like Jell-O), but the water may not completely cover the bones, depending on the size of the pot and how the bones are cut. Exposed bones above the water line do not add flavor to a stock during cooking and may dry out, adding bitterness. Slightly increasing the amount of water to bones resolves this problem.

Basic professional stock recipes (Recipe 1-4) include water, bones, vegetables, herbs, and seasonings to develop flavor. White stock uses a two to three (2:3) ratio of bones to water. For a recipe that yields two gallons of stock, fifteen pounds of bones, and twenty-two and one-half pounds of water (~3 gallons) are used. The recipe yield is about thirty percent less than the starting amount of water. The water loss is due to evaporation during cooking and the removal of bones, aromatics, and flavorings at the end of cooking. The aromatics are referred to as *mirepoix* (meer-pwa), a French term for a mixture of onions, carrots, and celery. These aromatics are generally used in a ratio of two-to-one-to-one (2:1:1) or 50 percent onions, 25 percent carrots, and 25 percent celery (Professional Chef, 2011). The three pounds of *mirepoix* in the recipe equals one and one-half pounds of onions and three-quarters of a pound each of carrots and celery.

Note that the total amount of the *mirepoix* is 20 percent of the weight of the chicken bones. The herbs and seasonings add little weight to the recipe. A *sachet* is a blend of aromatic ingredients tied in a cheesecloth bag and added to the stock during cooking.

For the home cook, the two-gallon recipe yield is probably larger than necessary. One quart of stock is likely more appropriate (Recipe 1-5). Maintaining a ratio of two-to-three (bones to water), two pounds of bones requires three pounds of water.

Two pounds of bones is the approximate yield from deboning three, three-pound whole frying chickens. Since fluid ounces and dry ounces are not the same, three pounds of water is about six cups. The amount of *mirepoix* needed is six ounces or 20 percent of the weight of the chicken bones. Using the ratio for *mirepoix*, three ounces of onions and one and a half ounces each of carrots and celery are needed.

These white stock ratios also apply to the development of veal or beef stock. Knowing the quantity of bones on hand, the corresponding amount of water can be added in a two to three ratio (2:3) to yield a flavorful stock. There is a practical limit to how small or large a recipe can be scaled using ratios. Making

Recipe 1-4

Basic Chicken Stock (Yield 2 gallons)

Ingredients

15 lb.	chicken bones
22.5 lb.	cold water (~3 gallons)
3 lb.	*mirepoix*

2	bay leaves	
1 tsp.	thyme, dried	
1 tsp.	peppercorns, crushed	Sachet
8	parsley stems	

Method

1. Place the bones in a stockpot and cover them with the cold water. Bring the water to a boil and skim off the impurities.
2. Lower the heat to a simmer (185º F) and add the *mirepoix* and *sachet*.
3. Simmer and skim the stock as necessary for 8 to 12 hours partially covered.
4. Strain, cool and refrigerate.

Recipe 1-5

Basic Chicken Stock (Yield 1 Quart)

Ingredients

2 lb.	chicken bones
3 lb.	cold water (~6 cups)
6 oz.	*mirepoix*

1/2	bay leaf	
1/8 tsp.	thyme, dried	
1/8 tsp.	peppercorns, crushed	Sachet
1	parsley stems	

Method

1. Place the bones in a stockpot and cover them with the cold water. Bring the water to a boil and skim off the impurities.
2. Lower the heat to a simmer (185º F) and add the *mirepoix* and *sachet*.
3. Simmer and skim the stock as necessary for 8-12 hours partially covered.
4. Strain, cool and refrigerate.

Figure 1-1 Measuring liquids in graduated glassware requires careful liquid alignment. Liquids measured on a scale in plastic cups do not require reference markings.

one quart of stock is almost too small a quantity for the recipe amounts, but it works if only a small amount of bones is available for use.

Ratios are not only used in the development of cold and hot foods, but also in professional baking and pastries where recipe ingredients are measured by their weight. Accuracy is important in products that are measured in very small or large amounts. In bread recipes, the amount of yeast can be measured down to three decimal places (.005 ounces), making teaspoon measures a poor choice.

On the other end of the spectrum, leveling off thirty-seven cups of flour takes too much time and is not a consistent measure. Ratios are not just used in production, but can be part of the recipe name. The 3-2-1 pie dough is not only great for pies and tarts, but the ratio is its name. The dough is made up of three (3) parts flour to two (2) parts fat to one (1) part water by weight.

Knowing the ratio, the recipe can be more easily scaled to yield different quantities. Additionally, weighing a fat like shortening is much easier than using a volume measure that requires scraping out with a spatula. Liquid ingredients can be measured with many different types of containers, such as plastic cups instead of traditional graduated glassware (Figure 1-1) that requires careful liquid alignment.

Ratios are best used when ingredients are weighed and not measured into cup and spoon measures. Volume measures can convey erroneous ingredient relationships that can lead to recipe errors. Ingredients vary in size and do not take up the same amount of space in a container. A grain of salt is not the same size as a whole peppercorn. Consequently, the number of salt grains in a teaspoon does not equal the same number of peppercorns in the same size measure. Establishing a ratio by the container size alone can therefore provide misleading information.

According to one Internet search result, cooking four cups of juneberries and three cups of sugar in a saucepan is one way to make juneberry jam. Based on the amount of cups used, there is a four to three (4:3) ratio between the juneberries and the sugar. The amount of juneberries appears to be greater than the quantity of sugar. Measured on a scale, four cups of juneberries weighs twenty ounces (20 oz.) and three cups of sugar weighs twenty-one ounces (21 oz.). By weight, the ratio between these ingredients is closer to one to one (1:1) and the amount of sugar is even slightly greater than the amount of berries.

For people who like sweet jam, these original amounts may be just fine. For others, knowing these relationships ahead of time facilitates recipe changes before cooking begins.

The weight of ingredients can be determined with a digital scale with an accuracy of .05 ounces for most ingredients. For yeast and other small quantities, a second scale with an accuracy of .005 ounces may have to be purchased.

Unfortunately, many digital scales from discount stores do not have these levels of accuracy or they display fractional amounts instead of their decimal equivalents. Digital scales can be found in stores, but Internet purchasing is likely more successful.

Jennings scales provide a high level of accuracy, have long warranties, and are durable for even professional use. Perhaps more convenient is to refer to *The Book of Yields* by Francis T. Lynch. This resource provides the weights of many herbs and spices, baking items, oils, and grains, among many other ingredients. Although no single resource can provide the weight of every possible ingredient, Lynch's work is comprehensive, even including the weight of rose blossoms.

Baker's Percentages in Bread Making

In bread making, the mathematical relationship between recipe ingredients is formalized in the baker's percentage system, where each ingredient is expressed as a percentage of the total weight of the flour (Hamelman, 2004). Using the weight of the flour as a point of reference for other recipe ingredients reflects its important role in the development of bread.

In this system, each recipe ingredient is divided by the weight of the flour to arrive at a percentage value. The flour's weight is assigned a value of one hundred percent. Using ingredient percentages increases production flexibility as the size of a batch can be scaled up or down depending on what ingredients are on hand. If there are eighteen ounces or ten pounds of flour available, a recipe can quickly be developed to reflect these amounts.

The use of the baker's percentage system also helps fix possible errors that include adding more flour than originally intended. In the following example (not an actual recipe), the amount of bread flour used is eighteen ounces. Therefore, this amount is given a value of 100 percent.

Quantity	Ingredient	Baker's Percentage
18 oz.	bread flour	(100%)
1 oz.	sugar	(5.5%)
.25 oz.	salt	(1.4%)
.15 oz.	instant yeast	(.83%)
1 oz.	oil	(5.5%)
3.3 oz.	eggs	(18.3%)
1.25 oz.	egg yolks	(6.9%)
7.5 oz.	water	(42%)

The remaining ingredients are then divided by the weight of the flour (eighteen ounces) to arrive at a dividend that is expressed as a percentage. Therefore, the weight of the sugar (one ounce) is divided by the weight of the flour (eighteen ounces) to arrive at an answer that is out of one hundred, commonly referred to as a percentage. This numerical answer is expressed as a percentage by moving the decimal point to the right two places.

1 ounce of sugar ÷ 18 ounces of flour = .055 or 5.5%

For most people, 5.5 percent is a more conventional way to show a percentage than the numerical equivalent of .055 that results from straight mathematical calculation. The rest of the ingredient values are determined by using the same method of division. After these percentages have been determined, they now can be used to determine new quantities of ingredients if the amount of flour changes.

Perhaps confusing at first, the baker's percentage system is an ingenious way to use a known quantity of flour to determine the quantities of the remaining recipe ingredients. If this system is making sense to you, twenty-four ounces of flour would require 1.32 ounces of sugar, .34 ounces of salt and .20 ounces of yeast, etc.

The baker's percentage system can also identify recipe problems early in the selection process where ingredient weight is provided. One common problem is the amount of water in bread recipes. Breads like ciabatta contain a lot of water, while others, such as basic French bread, do not. The phrase "a lot of water" is hard to quantify using cup and spoon measures but is readily identifiable using baker's percentages.

According to Reinhart (2001), the amount of water in ciabatta can range from 65 percent to 80 percent, with French bread anywhere from 55 to 65 percent. If the amount of water in a French bread recipe is calculated to be 80 percent of the weight of the flour, there may be a recipe error or further review may be needed.

For most consumer recipes, ingredient conversion to ounces is necessary before the baker's percentage system can be applied. The results of this work are shown for an Internet recipe for Basic French Bread (Recipe 1-6). Once this

---

Recipe 1-6

Basic French Bread (Yield 2 large loaves)

Ingredients

Amount	Ounces	Percent	
6 C	27.6 oz.	100%	AP Flour
2 ½ pkgs.	.63 oz.	2 %	active dry yeast
1 ½ tsp.	.33 oz.	1%	salt
2 C	16 oz.	58%	water

work is completed, the percentages of flour can be calculated for recipe ingredients. Originally in cup and spoon measures, the recipe ingredients have been converted to ounces and the baker's percentages have been calculated.

The weight of the water is 58 percent of the weight of the flour, which falls within the norms of French bread hydration. If the amount of water had been a half a cup more (2½ cups instead of 2 cups), the percentage would climb to 72 percent, outside the normal range.

Does this finding make this a good-tasting bread recipe? Looking at the hydration percentage alone does not answer this question but suggests some level of confidence in the recipe's development. The amount of yeast in bread is typically between 1 and 2 percent of the weight of the flour; at 2 percent, this bread falls on the high side of that norm.

Changing Recipe Yields

Recipe yields sometimes have to be changed to produce a larger or smaller quantity. In consumer recipes, doubling or reducing a recipe by one-half is probably not an issue unless you are dealing with odd-sized measures, such as two-thirds of a teaspoon.

Changing the yield outside of these basic changes is difficult because consumer recipes typically lack the necessary information. Although the number of servings is usually provided, the recipe yield in ounces and the serving size are not provided. Together, these two factors indicate the number of people that can be fed and how much each person is expected to consume. Of these two factors, the serving size determines how much food to produce since the more a person eats, the less food that is available for others.

How do you figure out how much to make when people do not always eat the same amount? One way to answer this question is to frame the response in terms of the dining context. The word dining may suggest some kind of elegant affair, but dining can be less formal. In a highly mobile society, a business meeting or a small group tailgating at a sporting event could define dining. Of the many different dining contexts, guidelines used by restaurants provide a point of reference for discussion.

The entrée protein (meat) for a sit down dinner generally weighs from six to eight ounces for each person, with a lunch portion about three to six ounces.

If the protein includes bones, the weight of the protein increases to about eight to ten ounces per person for dinner.

Some restaurants will use much larger values, doubling the portion size or making them even larger. Side dishes like potatoes, rice, and pasta (starches) range from three to four ounces per serving. These same values can be used for vegetable sides like carrots, corn, or peas.

Another situation that many people face is having a large party with a buffet table of assorted dishes. In these situations, people tend to sample a smaller portion of the multiple options available. As the number of buffet offerings increases, the amount eaten of any one dish generally trends down. A plate can only hold so much on a trip through the line and not every person will go through multiple times.

The order of food placement also influences the amount eaten. People tend to take more of items located at the beginning of the line than those later in the order. As a starting point, expect each person to consume about a pound of total food from all the offerings available (Labensky & Hause, 2007).

Diverse offerings will reduce the serving size of any one item down to one-half to a quarter of what would be eaten if they were offered alone. For one hundred people, this would approximate two to three ounces of any given entrée, one to one and a half ounces of a starch, and one ounce of vegetables. People tend to eat more starches like pasta than vegetables like peas, corn, or carrots. The point to keep in mind is that people eat more of any one item if there are fewer options available.

What changes this approach is when a dish is known to be highly favored over the other offerings. In a Chinese buffet situation, people tend to flock to the General Tso's chicken over chicken in garlic sauce.

There are two common ways to change a recipe's yield. The first method changes the number of servings while keeping the serving size the same. In this example, the need is to feed a greater or smaller number of people but leave the amount they are expected to eat the same.

The recipe for Rotini salad (Recipe 1-7) yields twenty-seven ounces of salad, serves six people, and has a serving size of four and one-half ounces. The serving size is a good-sized portion that would be served along with other items on a lunch plate. If the number of servings required increased from six to ten, each person would now only be given a three-ounce portion (2.7 oz.), calculated by dividing the total yield by ten.

Recipe 1-7

Italian Tri-Colored Rotini Salad (Yield 27 ounces, 6- 4.5 ounce servings)

6 oz.	tri-color rotini, uncooked
6 oz.	artichoke hearts, canned
1.6 oz.	red pepper strips
5 oz.	broccoli florets
4 oz.	cubed mozzarella cheese
.23 oz.	parsley, chopped
4 oz.	Italian salad dressing
26.83 oz.	Total Yield

This reduced serving size may work in some situations, but if the serving size is to remain the same, additional salad needs to be made. The new yield for ten people is calculated by first determining a conversion factor that is then applied to each ingredient in the original recipe. The conversion factor is determined by dividing the new yield by the original yield.

(New Yield ÷ Original Yield) = Conversion Factor

In this formula, the original yield is already known and is twenty-seven ounces. Since this is a professional recipe, this yield information is found to the right of the recipe name. The new yield is determined by multiplying the desired number of new servings by the serving size that remains the same. In this case, ten servings are needed, which represents four more than the original quantity.

(Number of Servings Required X Serving Size) = New Yield
(10 Servings Required X 4.5-ounce Serving Size) = 45 ounces

Multiplying the new number of servings by the original serving size increases the recipe yield to forty-five ounces. Having determined the new yield, the conversion factor can now be calculated by dividing the new yield by the recipe's original yield.

(New Yield ÷ Original Yield) = Conversion Factor

(New Yield 45 ounces ÷ Original Yield 27 ounces) = 1.7

The resulting conversion factor tells you that the new yield is 1.7 times greater than the original yield. This answer also sounds reasonable since the new number of servings is almost double the original six-serving yield. The next step is to multiply the conversion factor by each ingredient in the original recipe to arrive at the new quantity required. The new value for the rotini is calculated below:

(Original Ingredient Quantity X Conversion Factor) = New Quantity
(6 ounces of rotini X 1.7 Conversion Factor) = 10.2 ounces of rotini

When all the ingredients have been converted in this manner, the revised recipe (Recipe 1-8) contains these new ingredient amounts with adjustments made to the yield and number of servings. The new recipe yields forty-five ounces with ten servings, but keeps the serving size at the original amount. Having adjusted the recipe to feed ten people, new quantities of ingredients can be measured or purchased as necessary.

The second method to change a recipe's yield modifies both the number of servings and the serving size. This approach is used when the number of people being served changes, as well as how much each person is going to eat. Buffet planning is a good example where both the number of servings and the serving size change. Additional servings are necessary to meet the needs of a larger group of people. Adjustments to the serving size are also needed since

---

Recipe 1-8

Italian Tri-Color Rotini Salad (Yield 45 ounces, 10 - 4.5 ounce servings)

10 oz.	tri-color rotini, uncooked (6 oz. x 1.7 = 10.2 oz.)
10 oz.	artichoke hearts (6 oz. x 1.7 = 10.2 oz.)
3 oz.	red pepper strips (1.6 oz. x 1.7 = 2.72 oz.)
8 oz.	broccoli florets (5 oz. x 1.7 = 8.5 oz.)
7 oz.	cubed mozzarella cheese (4 oz. x 1.7 = 6.8 oz.)
.4 oz.	parsley, chopped (.23 oz. x 1.7 = .39 oz.)
7 oz.	Italian salad dressing (4 oz. x 1.7 = 6.8 oz.)
45.4 oz.	Total New Yield

people will likely eat less of any one item.

Fortunately, some of the concepts used in the previous example also apply to this second method to change the recipe yield. As before, the use of original and new yields determines a conversion factor that is applied to calculate new ingredient amounts.

$$(\text{New Yield} \div \text{Original Yield}) = \text{Conversion Factor}$$

The original rotini salad recipe (Recipe 1-7) served six people and had a serving size of four and one-half ounces. The original yield was twenty-seven ounces. In this buffet example, both the number of servings and the serving size will change. The number of servings generally reflects the number of people being served. If each person eats one serving, the number of servings equals the number of people being served.

Eighty people are expected to attend a buffet style college graduation party that will serve multiple offerings of an entrée, starch, and vegetable. With multiple starches being offered on the buffet table, a one and a half ounce (1.5 oz.) serving size of rotini salad is chosen over the original four and a half ounce (4.5 oz.) serving size. Having made a decision on the number of servings needed (80) and the serving size (1.5 oz.), the new yield can now be calculated by multiplying these two values together:

$$(\text{New Number of Servings} \times \text{New Serving Size}) = \text{New Yield}$$
$$(\text{New Number of Servings 80} \times \text{New Serving Size 1.5 oz.}) = 120 \text{ ounces}$$

Having determined the new yield (120 oz.) and knowing the original recipe yield (27 oz.), the conversion factor can now be calculated by dividing these values by each other.

$$(\text{New Yield} \div \text{Original Yield}) = \text{Conversion Factor}$$
$$(\text{New Yield 120 ounces} \div \text{Original Yield 27 ounces}) = 4.44$$

The conversion factor represents a four-time increase in the amount of rotini salad over the original quantity. Each ingredient in the original recipe is now multiplied by the conversion factor to determine the revised amount needed. The calculation of the rotini pasta follows:

Recipe 1-9

Italian Tri-Color Rotini Salad (Yield 7.5 lb. or 80-1.5 oz. servings)

27 oz.	tri-color rotini, uncooked (6 oz. x 4.44 = 26.64 oz.)
27 oz.	artichoke hearts (6 oz. x 4.44 = 26.64 oz.)
7 oz.	red pepper strips (1.6 oz. x 4.44 = 7.10 oz.)
22 oz.	broccoli florets (5 oz. x 4.44 = 22.20 oz.)
18 oz.	cubed mozzarella cheese (4 oz. x 4.44 = 17.76 oz.)
1 oz.	parsley, chopped (.23 oz. x 4.44 = 1.02 oz.)
18 oz.	Italian salad dressing (4 oz. x 4.44 = 17.76 oz.)
120 oz.	Total New Yield

(Original Ingredient Quantity x Conversion Factor) = New Quantity
(6 ounces of rotini X 4.44 Conversion Factor) = 26.64 ounces

The revised recipe (Recipe 1-9) yields seven and a half pounds of rotini salad that serves eighty people with a one and a half ounce (1.5 oz.) serving size. If the portion size had been used from the original recipe (4.5 ounces), the amount produced for eighty people would yield almost twenty-three pounds. This amount is three times larger than the revised yield calculated using the smaller one and a half ounce serving size.

Seven and a half pounds of salad may not seem like a lot for eighty people, but considered together with other planned offerings, the amount may not be as small as it seems. If the amount still seems too small, a different serving size could be used in the formula to determine any number of resulting greater yields. The right yield is the one you choose to develop and test that is confirmed by how much your guests consume. Evaluating the outcome informs future recipe revisions for the same or different group of people.

Determining Nutrient Food Values

The nutritional value of prepackaged foods is easily found on Nutrition Facts labels that contain both the number of servings and serving size information. Serving sizes are standardized to make comparing similar foods easier (FDA,

---

Recipe 1-10

Citrus Salsa (Servings 4)

Ingredients

2	navel oranges, segmented and diced
1	Roma tomato, seeded and diced
1 tbsp.	cilantro, chopped
1 tbsp.	jalapeno, minced
1 tbsp.	lime juice
To Taste	salt and pepper

Directions
Remove the skin of the orange. Cut into segments using the connective membrane as a guide. Seed the tomato and dice along with the orange segments. Add remaining ingredients and season to taste with salt and pepper.

Per serving: 49 cal; 0.13g total fat (0.03g salt); 0mg chol; 148mg sodium; 12.52g carb; 2.42g fiber; 1.18g protein; 8.32g sugars; 57.79mg Vitamin C

2014) and are stated in common measures such as cups, followed by their equivalent weight in grams.

The serving size is important, as the amount a person consumes influences the intake of calories and nutrient amounts. Unfortunately, these Nutrition Facts standards are not always part of consumer recipes that attempt to provide nutritional information. Often, the number of servings is shown, but not the serving size. As exacting as the nutrient values may appear to be in a recipe, without the serving size, the information is no more than an estimate since the user must guess at the size of a single serving.

Additionally, specific quantities may not be provided for some ingredients, such as salt and pepper, making nutritional information even more of a guess. One such example is a recipe for Citrus Salsa (Recipe 1-10) that was taken from a cooking magazine. The nutritional summary states that the amount of sodium per serving is 148mg, but the amount of salt in the recipe is variable, being "To Taste" (TT) and is not specifically provided. Also, the recipe does not provide a serving size so the user does not know how much of the salsa to consume in order to obtain the stated sodium values.

The yield of this recipe is also hard to determine since different-sized oranges, tomatoes, and jalapeno peppers produce a different quantity of salsa. These issues could be corrected in part by providing the weight of these ingredients. Their weight is a more precise and consistent measure than the variable size of a fruit or vegetable. If all the ingredients in the recipe were weighed, then a total recipe yield in pounds or ounces could be determined, along with a specific serving size that relates to the nutritional information provided.

Since recipes do not come with Nutrition Facts labels and many recipes do not provide nutritional information, how can nutrient values be determined? Fortunately, the United States Department of Agriculture has a free online nutritional database that provides information for a wide range of ingredient types, including raw, cooked, and packaged forms (NDL, 2013). Type in a food ingredient and its nutritional values are provided.

As an example, celery contains more sodium than raw cashew nuts. According to the online database, celery has 80mg/100g of sodium and cashew nuts have 12mg/100g. Since celery is a vegetable, the higher salt content in it may seem surprising.

Having this nutritional information can be quite helpful for people who want to take the time and watch what they eat. The USDA nutritional database is an excellent resource, but food values need to be searched one at a time. Looking up more than a few ingredients can be time-consuming. For those who have access to a computer, there are inexpensive software options that not only store recipe information, but perform nutritional analysis as well.

On the Apple Macintosh, MacGourmet Deluxe is an application that calculates nutritional information based on each ingredient and the amount used (Mariner Software, 2013). The software calculates food values using the same USDA nutritional database but can calculate the combined nutritional values for all recipe ingredients at one time. And new items can be added if an ingredient is not in the government's database. Although some ingredients are not included, such as oyster and fish sauces, farro, and agave nectar, these items are sold commercially and contain nutrition fact labels whose values can be entered into the MacGourmet database.

Making changes to a recipe's ingredients and its number of servings is not difficult and a click of a button recalculates nutritional outcomes. There are also versions for the popular Apple iPhone and iPad. For people using Microsoft Windows, Living Cookbook by Radium Technologies (Recipe Software, 2013) or MasterCook by Cosmi Finance, LLC, are options to explore.

What You've Been Missing in Recipe Development

Recipes are instruction sets that direct us on how to prepare food items. Because recipes are a set of directives, correct recipe execution is the focus of many efforts instead of considering what lies behind what is written. What is missing may be as important as what is revealed. Without access to the recipe author, knowing these hidden considerations is difficult but not impossible with a little sleuthing and applied knowledge.

When recipe outcomes do not produce the expected results or quantities cannot be scaled to meet varying needs, the problem may be with the recipe. Since recipes are sometimes shrouded in an air of mystery, knowing these recipe basics can help in recipe selection and changing outcomes to meet personal needs. What is missing from recipes?

- Chefs adapt their standardized recipes to meet the needs of the home cook since recipes are not all intended for consumer use.

- Consumer recipes are written for the home cook who may or may not have any culinary training. Recipes are designed to cook in short periods of time and not take long to prepare. Volume containers such as cups and spoons are used to measure ingredients to coincide with home kitchen conditions.

- Consumer recipes indicate the number of servings produced but typically not their yield by weight or the serving size.

- Professional recipes are designed for people with some level of culinary training and/or academic degrees. Recipes are characterized by their consistency. Their yields are designed to meet the needs of larger groups of people. Ingredients are often measured by their weight on a scale. Recipe yield, the number of servings, and the serving size are provided to assist with recipe changes.

- Standardized recipes are used in professional kitchens that take into account the specific working conditions. These recipes are not provided to consumers or published in cookbooks.

- Ingredients form comparative relationships known as ratios that can be used to develop foods or check amounts against known standards.

- Baker's percentages are used in the development of breads, where each ingredient is expressed as a percentage of the weight of the flour. These percentages can be used to change recipe yields or determine if ingredient amounts are outside accepted norms.

- The amount people eat depends in part on the dining context. Generally accepted restaurant standards for portion size can be used to determine the size of entrées, starches, and vegetables sides.

- As the number of food offerings increases in a buffet situation, the less of any one dish people will eat.

- Recipe yields can be increased or decreased by changing the number of servings while keeping the serving size the same. This approach can be used for large dinner parties where each person is expected to eat the same amount of the dish being prepared.

- Recipe yields can be increased or decreased by changing both the number of servings and the serving size. This approach is useful in buffet situations where the number of people served varies and the amount each person eats changes due to the diversity of foods being offered.

- Nutrient food values can be determined individually using Federal Internet resources or collectively in recipes using software options such as Mac Gourmet Deluxe and Living Cookbook.

RECIPES

Chapter Two

Reading Recipes
Interpreting Recipe Directions

Since recipes are written for both consumers and professionals, their level of explanation can vary greatly. Recipes may have a sentence or two on how to proceed from preparation to completion, while others contain a lot of detail.

Other times, recipe directions may reference a cooking method, but they really mean another. The word sauté is bandied about in recipes, sometimes referring to the cooking method and other times the cooking pan. Pan-frying in oil can be incorrectly referred to as a sauté since a sloping-sided sauté pan (*sauteuse*) is sometimes used.

Recipe omissions are more problematic because the home cook may not even know something is missing. In reality, following what the recipe says is not always the best guide to producing the desired outcome. In many cases, some level of recipe interpretation is required to "read between the lines" and prior experience flags possible errors.

Correcting for inconsistencies comes naturally after many years of dealing with and fixing recipe problems. Recipe inconsistencies in hot foods can be corrected by comparing known culinary methods to what is written in a recipe. Identifying methods that are far afield from culinary standards raises a red flag about the recipe's integrity.

Recipe errors can be fixed by applying the correct method or choosing another recipe. Taking things a step further, concepts from professional recipes can be applied to analyze and develop alternative recipes that produce better results. Basic hot foods cooking methods are reviewed in this chapter and sample recipes are analyzed and developed. Through these examples common places for recipe errors are identified to aid future recipe selection.

Cooking Methods and Techniques

Recipes are made up of ingredients, techniques, and cooking methods. Of these three components, techniques and methods are often used interchangeably in consumer recipes. In professional recipes, cooking methods may use techniques in their development, but the two are not one and the same.

In the context of recipe directions, deciphering which ones are methods and which are techniques avoids carrying out the wrong procedure. Is a sauté used to brown steaks or is the meat seared on both sides? The first is a cooking method that would not be used to brown steaks. The second is a technique that is used to form a crust on the meat exterior. The sauté method uses a sloping-sided pan to toss its contents, but a sear can be performed using the same pan type. Framing this discussion differently, steaks are not sautéed but can be browned on both sides in a sauté pan using the technique of searing that forms a crusting on the outside of the protein.

Cooking techniques refer to how recipe ingredients are prepared and involve a learned skill such as knife cutting, meat fabrication (butchering), or even flipping an egg omelet. Cooking methods refer to how ingredients are cooked to safe eating temperatures, not just prepared. They also describe the overall recipe approach and are sometimes referred to in the recipe name, such as Braised Short Ribs.

Cooking with heat is an important aspect that distinguishes the basic cooking methods from other approaches that make food safe to eat without the use of heat.

Some of these approaches involve chemical processes that break down or denature the proteins of animal flesh. Ceviche, for example, uses an acid such as lemon juice, to "cook" seafood such as shrimp. Fish that will be served raw or partially cooked can also be frozen for a time and at a specific temperature to kill any parasites that may be present (ServSafe, 2008). Ceviche and freezing are both safe ways to prepare food to eat, but they are not considered basic cooking methods.

Foods can be cooked in heated air, fat (oil), water, or steam generated by a heat source such as a flame or an electric element. Basic cooking methods are divided into dry-heat, moist-heat, or combination methods. Dry-heat methods cook foods with hot air or fat and create flavor through browning. Moist-heat methods cook foods by submerging them in a hot liquid or through the use of steam that tenderizes and brings out the natural flavors of the food.

Combination methods use both dry-heat and moist-heat methods to cook foods, effectively taking advantage of both flavoring methods. There are eight basic dry-heat, four moist-heat and two combination-cooking methods.

Dry-Heat Cooking Methods

Sautéing is a common dry-heat cooking method. Foods are typically tossed in a sloping-sided pan with a small amount of hot fat. High temperatures are used and an elliptical pattern of tossing causes the ingredients to jump and redistribute on the pan bottom. Ingredient browning is difficult if the pan is not allowed to rest on the heat source for a time in between tosses.

Attempting to sauté too many items at one time, referred to as overloading, causes the ingredients to steam instead of brown. Recipe directions may refer to this method as a shaking of the pan or mixing of ingredients. A variation of the sauté method is stir-frying that uses even higher levels of heat and a steel wok that has strongly sloping pan sides.

Confusion sometimes results from recipes that make use of a sauté pan but not the sauté method. The sweating technique often uses a sauté pan, but does not involve high heat or browning. Ingredients are cooked over low heat and covered until the item softens. The term *sweating* is used less commonly in recipes in favor of the words *cook until softened, translucent* or sometimes *lightly browned* (Figure 2-1). Perhaps *sweating* in the kitchen creates the wrong kind of visual image.

Broiling is a dry-heat cooking method familiar to many people who have home ovens that include built-in broiler units or broiling capacity. Broiling is distinguished by the location of an overhead heat source to cook foods. Heated air, not the flame of the broiler, cooks the food. For attractive crosshatch marks, a slotted grate can be placed under the food during cooking.

Figure 2-1 Sweating is a cooking technique that is often done in a sauté pan, but does not use the sauté technique. Sweated onions are translucent instead of dark brown.

Commonly broiled foods are fish, meats, and vegetables. Usually this technique is referred to by its correct name. The distance maintained between the flame and the food during cooking is not always provided, but typically ranges from two to four inches. Recipes that provide a distance measure demonstrate knowledge of the method and will probably have a higher level of success. Make sure the broiler is preheated before cooking the item.

Grilling is a dry-heat method that is sometimes confused with broiling since grilled foods can also be marked with attractive crosshatching during cooking. The heat source for grilling is located beneath the food and not on top as in broiling. Food cooks from the conduction of heated air from a source that is typically a flame. Cast iron grill pans are also used to create crosshatch marks on foods. Sometimes referred to as *grilling*, this use of the term is incorrect. Heat is not transferred through the air as in grilling, but from flame to pan bottom and to the food directly. To keep food from sticking to a grill's surface, heat then clean and oil the surface before cooking food. Cleaning a heated grill is easier than when the grill surface is cold.

Barbecuing is another dry-heat method, where foods are often cooked in the smoke of an open flame, traditionally from wood sources. Grilling is sometimes confused with barbecuing because people grill meat like hamburgers in what is commonly called a barbecue.

Roasting and *Baking* are dry-heat cooking methods where foods are surrounded by the dry heat of an enclosed environment, like an oven. Although the cooking method is the same for both, roasting usually refers to meats and poultry, while baking commonly refers to bread, pastries, fish, vegetables, and fruits. Normally, we do not refer to bread being roasted in an oven, but rather being baked.

Pan-frying is another common dry-heat cooking method. Foods are cooked in a moderate amount of heated fat that partially surrounds the food. A sauté pan can be used to pan-fry foods, but pan-frying is different from the sauté technique. Foods are typically breaded and placed in hot fat that is one-third to halfway up the item's sides--an important point that is sometimes omitted in recipes. The fat used is also at a lower temperature than is used in the sauté technique. Turning the item half way through cooking is part of the method to brown both sides. The tricky part about pan-frying is not heating the fat to such a high temperature that the outside of an item browns and the inside remains uncooked. If the opposite occurs and the fat temperature is too low, the item will absorb more fat than is necessary. Pan-frying may appear to be easy, but heat control is important to its success.

Deep-frying is the last basic dry-heat cooking method that involves heat transfer to foods submerged in hot fat. Not often mentioned in recipe directions is the necessary instruction to place foods in hot oil with your hand motion away from you. The oil splash will then be away from your body, helping to avoid oil burns. Dropping a food item in hot fat directly will cause oil to backsplash onto you.

Mini deep fryers today come with built-in temperature controls and wire baskets that can be used to cook items that are frozen or do not stick together easily.

Battered items that would sink and stick to the basket's wire frame can be cooked using the swimming method. Food is lowered partway into the hot fat and released carefully to avoid oil splash onto your hands. The battered item will initially sink but will rise (swim) to the oil's surface as it cooks. When the side that is in contact with the oil is properly browned, the food is turned over using a pair of tongs. Japanese tempura is cooked using the swimming method.

Moist-Heat Cooking Methods

Poaching and *Boiling* are two moist-heat cooking methods that are sometimes confused. These methods both use a hot liquid to cook ingredients. These liquids can include water, fruit juices, butter, and other aromatic liquids, such as a French court bouillon. Heat transfer from the surrounding liquid to the food cooks both poached and boiled items.

Poaching temperatures typically range from 160° F to 180° F, far below the boiling point (212° F) of water. Poaching is a good method for cooking delicate items like eggs or soft items like fish or fruit. Boiling these items will cause them to break up or become tough and stringy. Foods can be fully submerged or poached in liquid that comes halfway up the item's sides.

Consumer recipes often advocate bringing the poaching liquid to a boil before adding the item to be cooked. Boiling liquids may make cooking faster and be easier to recognize but boiling may not be necessary. Poaching temperatures below 160° F can also be used to cook some seafood items.

According to government guidelines, shrimp as seafood is cooked at 145° F, and cooking at 212° F or even 160° F can raise the internal temperature well beyond what is required. Poaching at these temperatures overcooks the shrimp and at 212° F makes its flesh rubbery. Starting the poach liquid at 145° F and allowing the internal temperature of the shrimp to come to that temperature cooks the protein but prevents overcooking by over sixty degrees. This method is not for everyone and takes skill and practice, but it is mentioned to show how poaching can result in tender foods.

Simmering is very common in recipes and lies between poaching and boiling temperatures. Simmering temperatures are between 185° F and 205° F. Simmering is often used to tenderize less tender cuts of meat like poultry through a long and slow cooking process. Simmered foods are submerged in a hot liquid and held at temperature. Simmering is sometimes confused with a boil in consumer recipes.

Steaming is the last basic moist-heat cooking method. Steaming cooks food through the transfer of heat from the steam to the food. As in poaching, the liquid that is used to steam foods can be flavored as well and includes wine, stock, or fruit juice. Steaming is commonly associated with delicate foods, such as fish and vegetables.

Combination Cooking Methods

Braising incorporates both dry-heat and moist-heat methods. Foods that are braised are usually large cuts of meat that are tenderized in the process. Pot roast and short ribs are good examples of meats that are typically cooked using the braise technique.

Braised meat is initially flavored through the Maillard Reaction named after Louis Camille Maillard, who discovered and described them in the early 20th century (McGee, 2004). High temperatures and the dry-heat environment of a lightly oiled pan change meat proteins and naturally occurring sugars into a browned and intensely flavored result. This browning reaction is different from caramelization that takes place with carbohydrates like sugar. Chefs who refer to meat browning as caramelization use the term incorrectly or perhaps choose to use a word that is more recognizable by the home cook.

After browning, the meat is cooked in a liquid along with vegetables and seasonings for the remainder of the cooking time. The slow moist-heat cooking tenderizes the meat. The protein is not completely covered by the liquid. This action may seem counterintuitive due to fears that the meat will not cook or will dry out unless completely covered by liquid. A tight-fitting lid keeps the moisture from escaping too quickly. Basting and turning during cooking helps keep the meat from drying out. The liquid is strained after the meat has finished cooking and makes an accompanying sauce that complements the food.

Stewing is a combination method that cooks smaller-sized or cut-up pieces of meat. Similar to a braise, the protein is browned in a little bit of fat and cooked in a liquid that also serves as a sauce. Unlike the braise method, the pieces of protein are completely covered by the liquid and simmered at a constant temperature until tender.

Identifying Recipe Methods and Techniques

Reading recipe directions is often an adventure into the unknown. You never know what to expect because the unexpected is the norm. Five star rating systems may provide some indication of recipe quality but, depending on the sample size, the rating may not be representative of the outcome.

Without recipe standards, any number of approaches can be taken and cooking methods and techniques can be described in a variety of ways. Reading other people's opinions can be helpful, but reading the recipe from beginning to end may be more useful. Identify and make a mental or written note of the methods and techniques used in the recipe. Then look for errors in sequencing or in the description of techniques.

Browning meat after cooking has finished would be out of sequence in braises. Sweating onions over high heat to brown them is an error in technique. Is guidance continually provided or are big leaps made between recipe procedures? These gaps represent areas that the author assumes the reader is able to fill in on their own. In some cases, people know what is missing; other times research is needed to fill in the blanks.

Common sense and your gut reaction will often take you down the right path. If something does not seem right, there probably is a reason why and it usually relates to how something is done or in its application in a recipe. This identification and analysis work is not an easy task, but it gets easier through many recipe successes and failures. Generally speaking, consumer recipes are likely to describe methods and techniques incorrectly. Professional recipes do not provide enough detailed information.

Recipes generally contain more techniques than cooking methods since foods can be prepared in many ways but are cooked by only a handful of methods. A good place to begin the search for cooking methods is in the recipe name. Braised Beef with Red Onion Gremolata, Sautéed Green Beans with Garlic and Herbs, and Boiled Potatoes with Butter state the cooking method. If correctly titled, the reader should know immediately what is involved in cooking the dish.

From the name alone, you can tell that a recipe for Braised Saffron Chicken and Leeks (Recipe 2-1) needs to include both dry-heat and moist-heat cooking methods. The chicken should be browned first and then finished in a covered moist-heat environment. The directions indicate that the chicken is browned and cooked in a covered environment consisting of stock, wine, thyme, saffron, and bay leaves. These dry-heat and moist-heat methods validate the recipe method and verify its name.

If these methods are missing from the recipe, the title is incorrect and the recipe's actual cooking method will need to be determined. If the method is in error, the validity of everything else in the recipe should be questioned as well.

The second method used in the recipe is simmering. The chicken is simmered inside its covered, moist-heat environment. There are several techniques

---

Recipe 2-1

Braised Saffron Chicken and Leeks

Ingredients

olive oil
whole chicken, cut into 8 pieces
leeks - white part only (fine julienne cut)
garlic, minced
white wine and chicken stock
dried thyme, bay leaves, saffron threads
lemon juice, unsalted butter, parsley leaves - chopped
salt and pepper

Directions

Heat oil in a Dutch oven over medium-high heat. Season the chicken with salt and pepper and brown both sides, set aside. Pour off most of the fat, add the leeks and garlic. Lower the heat, cover and cook 5 minutes until softened. Deglaze the pan with wine. Add the stock, thyme, saffron and bay leaves. Return the chicken back into the pan and simmer covered for 30 minutes. Let the liquid reduce and thicken with the lid off. The chicken is done with the internal temperature of the breasts reach 165 ° F. Discard the bay leaves. Remove surface fat with a spoon. Take the Dutch oven off-heat and add the butter, lemon juice and parsley leaves. Adjust the seasonings as necessary and serve immediately.

---

implied or referenced in the recipe. The sweating of leeks is an implied technique. These vegetables are cooked, covered, in a low-heat environment until "softened."

Deglazing is a technique that removes the browned bits from the pan bottom. Reduction is a natural way to thicken a sauce through liquid evaporation and consequent concentration. Defatting is a technique that removes fat from the surface of the sauce. Knife-cutting techniques are needed to fabricate the chicken, julienne the leeks, mince the garlic and chop the parsley leaves.

Poaching is a popular moist-heat cooking method to prepare shrimp for cocktails and salads. The recipe for Lemon Poached Shrimp (Recipe 2-2) contains an inviting list of ingredients that include white wine, lemon juice, herbs, and seasonings. The recipe is from a fine cooking web site with a five star review. With ingredients that sound great together and a perfect score, everything about this recipe must be perfect!

Recipe 2-2

Lemon Poached Shrimp

Ingredients

jumbo shrimp, unpeeled
water
white wine
black peppercorns
bay leaves
kosher salt
lemon juice

Directions

Combine wine, water, peppercorns, bay leaves and kosher salt in a large pot. Gently squeeze the lemon halves over the liquid and drop in the halves. Bring the liquid to a boil over medium-high heat, reduce the heat to medium low and let simmer gently for 10 minutes. Add the shrimp, cover and poach for four minutes. Turn off the heat and let cook another two minutes. Transfer to a colander until they are cool enough to handle, about fifteen minutes.

The directions call for first bringing the ingredients to a boil. Poaching temperatures are way below 212° F, so the method described in the recipe is already in error. Reducing the heat and maintaining the liquid at a simmer still represents too high of a poaching temperature. The words "gentle simmer" in consumer recipes could mean anything but imply a low boil since the shrimp remains covered during "poaching." The covered environment does not allow built-up heat to escape. The shrimp are cooked for a total of six minutes, four minutes over heat and two minutes off-heat. This cooking time is incorrect, however, because the shrimps are not immersed (shocked) in ice water to stop the cooking process.

Cooking continues (carryover cooking) while the shrimp sit in a colander until they are cool enough to handle. According to the recipe, this could take about fifteen minutes. The total cooking time is actually up to twenty-one minutes. This cooking method does not reflect a true poach but rather some kind of adaptation that leads to overcooked shrimp.

Sautéing is a common dry-heat cooking method that is fun to watch on cooking shows where food is tossed in an elliptical pattern in a sauté pan. In

---

Recipe 2-3

Sautéed Pork Chops with Balsamic Onions

Ingredients

olive oil
red onion, thinly sliced
bone-in center-cut pork chops
kosher salt
black pepper
balsamic vinegar
thyme leaves

Directions

Heat oil in a large sauté pan over medium high heat. Add onions and cook, stirring frequently, until soft and caramelized, about 20 minutes (if the onions start to burn, reduce the heat to medium low). Transfer onions to a bowl.

Dry pork chops with paper towels and season both sides with salt and pepper. Return the pan to the burner; heat the oil and brown well on one side, 3 to 5 minutes. Turn and cook the other side until the meat is done, about 2 to 4 minutes. Tent with foil and set aside to keep warm.

Put the pan back over medium heat and add the vinegar and caramelized onions. Simmer until the vinegar is reduced and coats the onions. Stir in thyme and season with salt and pepper. Serve with the pork chops.

---

this context, a recipe for Sautéed Pork Chops with Balsamic Onions (Recipe 2-3) sounds a bit odd since sautéing pork chops would require tossing them repeatedly in a pan.

This recipe, like the previous one, comes from a cooking website and has a five star rating. The recipe directions begin with a sauté, but one that involves onions and not pork chops. Oil is heated over medium-high heat in a sauté pan. The onions are added and stirred frequently to caramelize their sugars. Frequent stirring in these conditions qualifies as a sauté even though the ingredients are not tossed elliptically in the pan. Stirring frequently is an easier, less technique-driven way to accomplish the same end.

The pork chops are browned well on one side turned and cooked on the other. The browned side is what people see when the pork chop is plated and is called the presentation side. Since the chops are not sautéed but are browned, the term sautéed in the recipe name refers to the pan used to cook the pork chops, not the cooking method. Although the manner in which the ingredients are cooked produces good results, the recipe name suggests a different cooking method from the one that was used to cook the chops.

Although cooking methods may make captivating recipe titles, cooking techniques are the backbone of well-prepared recipes. Since they are skill based, poorly executed techniques can be the undoing of an otherwise great recipe. When an outcome is not as expected, the problem could be with the execution of a technique and not an ingredient issue, which many people look to first. Buying an expensive steak and not searing the outside well enough to develop a good crusting makes for a less flavorful and visually unappealing experience.

Unfortunately, techniques are often glossed over in recipes with just a casual reference. Recipes that call for a diced onion rarely explain the dicing procedure. Cooking techniques are mostly found in the directions or methods section of a recipe, but they can be found or implied in the ingredient list as well. Knife skills to prepare both the vegetables and chicken for cooking were implied in the ingredient list of the Braised Saffron Chicken and Leeks (Recipe 2-1).

Cantonese Sweet and Sour Chicken (Recipe 2-4) is a technique-driven dish made up of crispy chunks of chicken breast in a flavorful sweet and sour sauce. Incorrectly associated with pineapple chunks, green peppers, and tomatoes, this dish contains only battered and deep-fried breast of chicken with an accompanying sauce (Wang, 2014).

The recipe's simple output, however, may downplay the importance of technique in the preparation of this dish. In practice, there are several cooking techniques that make this popular Cantonese dish a success. Knife techniques are used to slice the orange, lemon, and ginger that provide the sweet and sour flavor in the sauce. These knife skills are not referenced in the directions but are inferred in the ingredient list. Knife skills are specifically referenced in the directions to prepare the chicken and create evenly sized pieces for deep-frying.

A whisk, consisting of several wire loops joined at the handle, is used to blend, mix, and incorporate several ingredients to make the batter. Placing the coated chicken pieces into the hot oil using a toothpick is a technique that

---

Recipe 2-4

Cantonese Sweet and Sour Chicken

Ingredients

chicken breast, cut into 1" pieces
salt, white pepper, garlic powder
Shaoxing wine, vegetable oil
cornstarch
egg, water, flour
baking powder

orange, sliced 3/8" rounds
lemon, sliced 1/4" rounds
ginger, bias cut
sugar
vinegar
ketchup

Directions

For the sauce, bring the water to a boil in a large pot and add the orange, lemon and ginger slices. Boil for about 30 minutes until the volume of water is reduced by 50 percent. Strain out the fruit slices and ginger. Add the sugar, vinegar, and ketchup to the mixture and stir until well blended. Mix the cornstarch and water together and then add to the sauce to thicken. Set the sauce aside.

Cut the breast in half with the knife parallel to the board. Slice each of the breast halves lengthwise into thirds. Cut each strip diagonally into 1" pieces. Place the chicken pieces in a bowl and add the salt, white pepper, garlic powder, wine, oil and mix together well. Cover the bowl with plastic wrap and marinate in the refrigerator.

For the batter, combine the garlic powder, white pepper, salt, cornstarch, egg and water. Beat with a whisk until well blended and the mixture foams. Add one half of the flour and incorporate with a whisk. When well blended, add the remaining flour and whisk until a smooth batter forms. Add the oil and whisk again to incorporate. Lastly add the baking powder and mix well. The batter should be very thick.

Take the chicken out of the refrigerator, add to the batter and mix well. Heat the oil in a wok to 370° F. Use a toothpick to pick up each piece of chicken. Use your thumb to push the chicken into the oil low and away from you to avoid an oil splash. Deep-fry the chicken for about 2 minutes until slightly browned. Remove the chicken, drain, and rest for 30 seconds. Add the partially cooked chicken back into the hot oil and fry for another minute for an extra crispy batter. Drain and serve with the sauce.

---

creates the evenly shaped pieces that people associate with sweet and sour chicken.

Techniques play an important role throughout the recipe's development. Deep-frying and boiling may be the recipe's two major cooking methods, but many more techniques are necessary to make the recipe a success. Only by analyzing the recipe in its entirety can techniques be identified, since some are "hidden" in the ingredient list while others are found in the directions section. Simple-looking dishes may actually be the ones that take many steps to prepare and execute well.

Professionalizing Consumer Recipes

Professional recipe development is not limited to chefs and restaurants. Consumers can develop more consistent recipes by applying the concepts used in professional recipe development. Working with ingredient weight instead of volume reveals important relationships that lead to better outcomes. Calculating or looking up the weight of ingredients does take time, but the effort is worthwhile.

Cup measures are especially problematic when quantifying raw vegetables. The number of carrots that fits into a cup measure is variable. When the recipe indicates a measuring cup "filled with chopped carrots," the amount can refer to anything, since chopping is a random knife cut. The reference to "small" or "large" diced carrots is useful, but these terms imply something different to each person.

In contrast, professionally diced carrots are cut to a specific size and the terms *small* and *large* have meaning. Small diced carrots are one-quarter inch-sized cubes. Large diced carrots are one-inch in size. The size issue becomes more problematic in consumer recipes when dealing with raw vegetables that are expressed as a numbered amount, such as one cucumber or two carrots. Vegetables and fruits vary in size, yielding different results every time.

In recipes that contain only a few ingredients, vegetable size does matter. Carrot-based salad dressings are good examples, since their consistency is influenced by the ratio of carrots to the liquids in the recipe. Carrots are vegetables that vary greatly in size, depending whether they are sorted into plastic bags or sold separately in bulk bins.

Japanese carrot dressings have a consistency that is more like a ranch style or Thousand Island dressing than a French vinaigrette. This thicker texture is difficult to reproduce consistently when whole carrots are used. Recipes of this kind (Recipe 2-5) show up frequently on the Internet and often lead to inconsistent and confusing results. Looking at the ingredient list, the size of the

---

Recipe 2-5

Japanese Carrot Ginger Salad Dressing

Ingredients

4	carrots
½	white onion
¼ C	ginger, chopped
2 tbsp.	miso paste
¼ C	rice vinegar
2 tbsp.	honey
3 tbsp.	sesame oil
2 tbsp.	vegetable oil
¼ C	water
½ tsp.	salt
½ tsp.	pepper

Directions

Mix everything in a blender until smooth.

---

carrots is missing. The directions do not provide further insight into the carrot's size or weight, so the reader must determine these values on their own.

Ingredient conversion of whole carrots and onions can be done with a digital scale or with the help of the chart in Appendix I that contains the weight of many vegetables and fruits. Irregularly shaped root vegetables like ginger are difficult to measure and therefore need to be weighed on a scale. Although the skin, stem and root ends of some vegetables and fruits are discarded before use, the untrimmed weights provide a place to start.

Liquids are more difficult to convert since fluid ounces and dry ounces are not the same. In consumer recipes, water, wine, vinegar, and larger quantities of oil are quantified in fluid ounces. Weighing these ingredients on a scale can be done but may not be necessary indivdually. Vinegar, wine, and stocks are made up of mostly water; therefore, the weight of water can be used instead of weighing these ingredients.

One fluid ounce of water equals 1.041 dry ounces (Wolfram Alpha, 2013). The difference between this weighed amount and one fluid ounce may not appear that significant. In small quantities this is correct. For one gallon of water, the difference is around five ounces. For small amounts or where precision is not needed, the number of fluid ounces can equal the number of ounces as measured on a scale.

The same can be said for small quantities of oils that in larger quantities would not equal their fluid ounce values. Francis Lynch's *The Book of Yields* can be used to provide the weight of other liquid ingredients like honey and other dry ingredients, such as the recipe's miso paste.

Different sizes of carrots and onions complicate the conversion of the Japanese Carrot Ginger Salad Dressing. With the recipe vegetables coming in large, medium, and small sizes, how can one size be chosen over the others? The choice can be arbitrary or reasoned out by comparing different recipe versions that use large-, medium-, and small-sized vegetables.

Three versions of the recipe are displayed, using a table format (Recipe 2-6). The rows and columns indicate different ingredient choices across recipe alternatives. The left column (Large) represents a version of the recipe that

---

Recipe 2-6

Japanese Carrot Ginger Salad Dressing

Large	Medium	Small	Ingredient
40 oz.	14 oz.	10 oz.	carrots
8.5 oz.	5.75 oz.	4.5 oz.	onion
3 oz.	3 oz.	3 oz.	ginger, chopped
1.2 oz.	1.2 oz.	1.2 oz.	miso (soybean) paste
(52.7 oz.)	(23.95 oz.)	(18.7 oz.)	**Total Vegetable Solids**
2 oz.	2 oz.	2 oz.	rice vinegar
1.5 oz.	1.5 oz.	1.5 oz.	honey
1.5 oz.	1.5 oz.	1.5 oz.	sesame oil
1 oz.	1.5 oz.	1.5 oz.	vegetable oil
2 oz.	2 oz.	2 oz.	water
(7 oz.)	(7 oz.)	(7 oz.)	**Total Liquids**
.11 oz..	11 oz.	.11 oz.	salt
.04 oz.	.04 oz.	.04 oz.	pepper
(.15 oz.)	(.15 oz.)	(.15 oz.)	**Total Seasonings**

Directions

Mix everything in a blender until smooth.

uses four large carrots (10 oz. each) and one-half of a large onion (17 oz.). The middle column (Medium) represents the recipe using medium-sized carrots and onions. The right column's (Small) recipe is based on the use of small carrots and onions. The amount of ginger and miso paste has been converted from cup and spoon measures to their equivalent weight values. Their amounts remain constant in all three versions to explore the effect vegetable selection has on the recipe's development.

Adding all the solids together in each version reveals large differences in the amount of dry ingredients used. The recipe version that uses large vegetables contains almost three times the amount of solids of the version that uses small vegetables.

Using large carrots and onions changes the recipe composition significantly. The amount of solids in all three versions far exceeds their liquids by over two times. The largest difference is over seven times greater when using large sized carrots and onions. When the vegetable solids far exceed the recipe liquids, the dressing will not hold together and its texture will be dry and crumbly. This analysis suggests that the amount of carrots has to be reduced or the amount of liquids increased, keeping the quantity of carrots the same.

At this point, progress is made through trial and error or by finding a different recipe that provides ingredient weight or at least provides volume measures for each ingredient type. Recipe conversion and analysis takes out some of the guesswork associated with recipe development and reveals potential problems before cooking begins. These are some of the benefits gained by incorporating aspects of professional recipe development into everyday consumer recipes.

The benefit of recipe conversion and analysis extends to other recipes of similar type. Chicken soup and white stock are both flavorful liquids where ratios play an important role. Classic Chicken Soup (Recipe 2-7) is basically a meat broth with onions, carrots, and celery. Chicken meat and bones are used in the soup's development and salt is added to enhance flavor. Converting the recipe ingredients to ounces reveals that the chicken and water are bascially in a one-to-one ratio.

Previously discussed in stock development, this relationship can be problematic, leading to ingredients that are not adequately covered by water. Recognizing this issue, the amount of water may need to be increased or the chicken cut into smaller pieces that allow them to be covered more easily. The onions,

---

Recipe 2-7

Classic Chicken Soup

Ingredients

Amount	Ounces	Item
4 lb.	64 oz.	whole frying chicken
8 C	67 oz.	water
1	17 oz.	large onion, quartered
3	10.5 oz.	carrots, 1" pieces
2	7 oz.	celery stalks, 1" pieces
2 ½ tsp.	.45 oz.	kosher salt
1 tsp.	.08 oz.	whole peppercorns
3	10.5 oz.	carrots, sliced rounds
2	7 oz.	celery, sliced

Directions

Place the chicken in a large pot along with the quartered onion, carrot and celery pieces, salt and pepper. Add enough cold water to cover the chicken (about 8 cups). Bring to a boil, skimming any foam that rises to the top. Reduce the heat to a simmer and cook until the chicken is done, about 45 minutes.

Transfer the chicken to a bowl and let cool. Strain the broth, discarding the cooked vegetables. Return the broth to the pot along with the sliced raw carrots and celery. Simmer the vegetables until tender, about 10 minutes. When the chicken is cool enough to handle, shred the meat and add to the soup.

---

carrots, and celery (*mirepoix*) are somewhat close to the same ratio used in stock development if medium-sized bagged carrots are used. The total amount of vegetables (34.5 oz.), however, is over 50 percent of the weight of the chicken. In chicken stock, where the flavor of the chicken leads over the aromatics, the *mirepoix* is 20 percent of the weight of the chicken. If the vegetable flavor is important in the broth, the recipe direction is a good one. If less vegetable flavors are desired, adjustments can be made, keeping the overall ratio of the *mirepoix* the same.

Completing the recipe interpretation is an analysis of recipe methods and techniques. Boiling and simmering are the two moist-heat cooking methods used to cook the chicken and make the broth. Since this is a consumer recipe, simmering probably equates to a low boil and not a true simmer that ranges between the temperatures of 185° and 205° Fahrenheit.

Knife techniques are used to prepare the vegetables and may have to be used to fabricate the chicken into smaller pieces if water amounts are not adjusted. Skimming is a technique that removes the chicken impurities as they rise to the liquid's surface.

Shredding the chicken by pulling the meat off the bones is a technique that gives the soup a rustic look compared to dicing the chicken into cubes. Although the overall methods and techniques are similar to stock development, the total cooking time is much shorter. Flavor development in such a short amount of time is limited.

Consumer recipes are designed for quick preparation and short cooking times. In this context, the forty-five-minute cooking time makes sense. For better chicken soup flavor, cooking times should be extended.

Converting the recipe ingredients and identifying the methods and techniques allows the user to analyze the recipe in its entirety and facilitates adjustments before cooking begins. This front-end work takes time but results in a product that better meets the needs and expectations of the user.

What You've Been Missing Reading Recipes

People follow recipe directions with the expectation that they will produce great results. Unfortunately, following these directives can lead to the unexpected. Without recipe standards, anything can be written and results vary. Reading recipes and following their directives is an act of faith that believes everything will turn out as expected. Recipe interpretation uncovers what is missing in recipe directions to prevent errors or avoids choosing a recipe that does not fill the expected need. What is missing from recipes?

- Cooking techniques refer to how recipe ingredients are prepared and are applied using a learned skill such as knife cutting.

- Cooking methods refer to how ingredients are cooked to safe eating temperatures and involve the use of a heat source.

- Consumer recipes consider cooking techniques and methods to be the same, which leads to confusion and errors in preparation and cooking.

- Professional recipes refer to cooking techniques and methods correctly but typically do not provide detailed information on their implementation.

- Recipes generally contain more techniques than cooking methods since foods can be prepared in many ways but cooked by only by a handful of methods.

- Cooking methods are divided up into dry-heat, moist-heat and combination cooking methods.

- When reading recipes, look for their techniques, methods, sequencing errors, and gaps between procedures.

- Cooking methods are sometimes included in the recipe name and should be confirmed in the directions or methods section.

- Combinations of flavorful ingredients work in conjunction with techniques and methods to produce great results. Ingredients in recipes do not function alone.

- Simple-looking foods may be the result of many techniques that require skill to execute well.

- Consumer recipes can incorporate aspects of professional recipes to make them better and more consistently reproducible.

- Converting ingredients from volume measures to their weight equivalents, as measured on a digital scale, reveals relationships that are otherwise hard to discern.

- The weight of water can be used to represent quantities of wine, vinegar, and stock that consist mostly of water. In small quantities or where precision is not important, fluid ounces and dry ounces can be used interchangeably.

- The table format works well to compare alternative versions of recipes where ingredient amounts vary.

- Ingredient conversion and analysis removes some of the guesswork associated with recipe development and reveals problems before cooking begins.

- Finding a new recipe may be a better course of action than committing to the development of one that has been discovered to have several errors.

- Similar types of recipes may share the same relationships between their ingredients, helping to identify problems.

RECIPES

Chapter Three

_____

Flavor Relationships
More Than Just Taste

Recipe ingredients, methods, and techniques work together to produce great-tasting food, but taste is only one aspect of an overall satisfying food experience. Food is not just tasted but is experienced with all the senses. Early in the morning, people's first food experience may not involve eating but smelling the aroma of freshly brewed coffee or toast browning. Hearing the sizzling sounds that come from bacon frying suggests to many that something good is being prepared.

Our sense of sight is a powerful force that influences what we choose to eat and our perception of food outcomes. Magazines and websites go to great lengths to make their recipe dishes look enticing. This photographic eye-candy attracts people and prompts them to make a particular recipe selection.

If the recipe outcome does not look like its stylized photo, the question of what went wrong comes to mind. The visual difference alone affects our perception of the food's characteristics. Our sense of touch determines a food's texture in our mouths. Ginger squash soup has a creamy texture and Pringles potato chips have that consistent crunch from batch to batch.

Together, taste, smell, sound, sight, and touch shape our food experiences. Of these influences, recipes primarily focus on the development of food that tastes, smells, and feels good in our mouths. Collectively, these three characteristics are called flavor. Flavor development is the focus of many kitchen discussions, television shows, books, and magazines. Chefs work toward building layers of flavors in foods and pairing complementary flavors.

This chapter deals with flavor's components and its development in recipes and points out flavor resources that are vanishing from the world around us.

Experiencing Flavor in Foods

Our perception of flavor develops overtime and evolves through many food experiences. Early in life, some people grow up in homes where there was always something cooking while others brought food in or ate out.

As people grow up to become adults, the foods they eat broaden their flavor horizons or confirm what they already know from past experience. Growing up with angel food cake from a box mix creates a preference for its flavor. Later in life, angel food cake made from scratch may not be preferred since its flavor is not the same as remembered. Going with what we already know is not a bad thing. Instead, these personal experiences contribute to our individual flavor palates.

The word *flavor* is loosely applied in everyday conversation. Flavor is made up of taste, aroma, and texture (Stuckey, 2013) but is commonly used to describe only one of these aspects. Salty-tasting soup is sometimes described as having a salty flavor. Is saltiness something people taste or a flavor in foods? Saltiness is a discernable taste and can also be a flavor enhancer. Salt used in Moroccan cuisine brings out the flavors of cinnamon that may otherwise be hidden in a dish (Goldstein, 1996).

Distinguishing between taste and flavor is difficult because they are are part of the same idea or two sides of the same coin. Additionally, ingredients may have a dominant taste but contain many flavors. Cumin has a bitter taste but can be described as pungent, earthy, or having the aroma of dirty feet. As a spice added to other ingredients and not eaten alone, cumin's texture does not really factor into its flavor. Bananas, on the other hand, have a soft or creamy texture, are sweet-tasting, and have a subdued flavor. Flavor's fullest expression is experienced through the process of eating but for our discussion is broken down into taste, texture, and aroma.

Figure 3-1 Tomatoes, basil and thyme contain less than 10mg/100g of sodium. Swiss chard naturally contains over twenty times more (213 mg/100g).

The complex nature of flavor is easier to understand when its component parts are discussed separately. Taste is the component that is probably most associated with flavor and is a good place to start the discussion. Tasting is done with our mouths that can distinguish saltiness, bitterness, sourness, sweetness, and a less-recognizable taste called umami (u-MOM-ee).

Saltiness in most recipes comes from the use of sodium chloride or table salt that also contains iodine to prevent its deficiency in the body. Kosher salt is used in the development of many hot foods since its larger particle size makes finger measuring (pinches) easier and hence more convenient to control.

Naturally occurring salts, such as Hawaiian red and Himalayan salts, also contain other minerals. Finishing salts like Fleur de Sel come in moist crystals or delicate flakes and are used sparingly to provide a burst of clean and mild flavor.

Some vegetables naturally contain a lot of sodium. Swiss chard, in the context of other commonly used vegetables and herbs, contains a great deal of sodium (Figure 3-1). Swiss chard contains 213mg/100g of sodium, tomatoes 5mg/100g, basil 4 mg/100g, and thyme 9mg/100g (Agricultural Research Service, 2013).

Bitterness is something that even in small amounts most people can readily identify. Common examples include bitter salad greens like arugula and endive but also foods that people enjoy every day like coffee, tea, and red wine. Spices like turmeric, thyme, and sage are also bitter-tasting but are not often described in this manner.

Bitter and sour tastes are sometimes confused since some sour foods, such as grapefruit, are also bitter. Sour tastes come from the acidity in the fruit, while bitterness is especially noticeable in the white part of the rind. Bitter and sour tastes can work together, however, when combined, as in tea with lemon.

Sourness is another taste that individually or at high levels is undesirable to some people. Drinking the juice from a lemon can be a mouth-puckering experience but can brighten up the flavor in foods because of the contrast lemon juice provides. Vinegar, another sour-tasting liquid that is not directly consumed, can be added to soups and meat sauces where its acidity cuts the apparent fattiness of the sauce.

Tomatoes and rhubarb are two vegetables that are also sour but do not come to mind as quickly as lemons and vinegar. Less known for their sourness are Cornelian cherry dogwood berries (*Cornus mas*). These fruits that resemble coffee berries are edible but very sour-tasting. Their sourness is somewhere between a cranberry and a sour cherry.

Sweetness is a taste that is easily recognized and favored by people. Commonly associated with sucrose or sugar, fruits such as grapes, apples, and pears naturally contain fruit sugar (fructose) that makes them taste sweet. Natural sweeteners such as honey, maple syrup, and agave nectar are used in many recipes. Sweetness is sometimes an end in itself, making its taste dominate a food as in powdered sugar donuts or some candies.

Umami is considered a fifth taste that some people may recognize, but its Japanese name is probably unfamiliar. The umami taste can be described as savory, satiating, or full. Umami-rich foods impart a deeper, weightier profile where a little can go along way to enhancing the taste of food. Umami refers to the taste of glutamates (amino acids) that are naturally found in some foods such as seaweed. These amino acids can also be found in common ingredients such as mushrooms. People who use soy or fish sauce, Parmesan cheese, or tomato ketchup can also experience the umami taste.

Meat proteins also contain umami-rich ingredients that are commonly formed through browning or in the curing of bacon and ham. Interestingly, white stocks contain umami's glutamates that are released during the long simmering of chicken and beef bones. The presence of these glutamates often makes stock a better choice in hot foods recipes that otherwise use water. Umami comes bottled in a jar but, like sour and bitter tastes, is unpleasant and is not eaten alone.

Known in Japan and sold in the United States as "Aji-no-moto" or more commonly "Accent," this white powder is a salt of glutamic acid that enhances the taste of foods. Also known by its chemical name Monosodium glutamate (MSG), this powder is sometimes used by restaurants in soups and on steaks. Although sodium is included in the name, MSG is not the same as table salt (sodium chloride) although its sodium compounds add to MSG's effectiveness.

Taste tends to get a lot of attention in recipe reviews, but aroma and texture are also important in determining the overall flavor of food. Maximizing food aromas is usually not considered a high priority in recipe development; nevertheless, they are part of a great flavor experience.

Imagine lemons, limes, and oranges without their citrus scent. The smell of breakfast cooking in the morning is perhaps more alluring than seeing or tasting the food once prepared.

The texture of food (mouthfeel) also plays an important role in flavor development. Chicken soup made with hard or mushy carrots would probably not be very flavorful. Frostings made with vegetable shortening can leave an oily feeling in the mouth that detracts from their flavor.

Serving temperature, spiciness, and astringency also contribute to the mouthfeel experience. Served on a cold wintery day, a bowl of cold chicken soup would be a flavor letdown. Spiciness may make food hot-tasting but not in reference to the food's thermal temperature.

Referred to as piquancy, spiciness is commonly associated with the use of Chili peppers. Strong flavors like Chilies and garlic, however, can be balanced (not sweetened) by the addition of honey, maple syrup, or fruit puree (Rapoport, 2014).

Astringency, or the feeling of having your tongue dry out, is also something people can detect in their mouths. Sometimes confused with bitterness, astringency is not a taste, but a mouthfeel. Some foods are both astringent and bitter-tasting at the same time, causing the confusion. Foods like coffee and tea contain astringent compounds (tannins) so they are both drying to the tongue and bitter at the same time. Astringency may be more easily identified in red wines that contain tannins but are also alcoholic beverages. Alcohol is an astringent. When alcohol dehydrates, the tongue feels dried out. This feeling is not the taste of bitterness. Differences like these make flavor a complex subject, one that is more than just taste, aroma, and texture individually. Flavor is experienced.

Flavor profiles are one way to capture and characterize these flavor experiences. These profiles describe a food's aroma, taste, and texture. Flavor profiles are difficult to determine in the context of life's many distractions. Checking for new messages on a smartphone and eating a sandwich at the same time may be multi-tasking, but probably does not serve either very well.

Despite modern conveniences, spending time on any one thing may be hard to accomplish. Simply slowing down and having the desire to experience what you are eating is one way to develop a deeper flavor understanding. Mentally, being present in the moment focuses the mind and effort on the flavor experience. The approach is not unlike wine-tasting that is more than a drink and a swallow. The experience unfolds along a continuum. The process begins with an initial upfront impression that unfolds further through eating and concludes with an impression at the end, sometimes referred to as the finish.

Our noses sense the aroma of food before eating even begins. These smells begin to shape the flavor experience and prepare our mouths for tasting. Smells continue to be a factor throughout the eating experience as they are released from the process of chewing. Aromas can be intently focused on, as in wine-tasting, or they can occur more naturally as the food is brought up to the mouth and chewed.

The flavor of chicken soup is first experienced through its aromas that are liberated through the evaporation of its broth. These volatiles are carried on the steam that rises from a hot bowl of soup, emphasizing the importance of food temperature. Tasting the soup likely forms a strong initial impression with other tastes being present, absent, or receding into the background.

Sweetness, that comes from the carrots that are crushed during chewing, may be experienced in chicken soup. Commercially canned chicken soup probably tastes very salty since salt is often a major component. After saltiness, the savory taste (umami) of the chicken broth may come through along with the soup's consistency. The texture could be watery, smooth, or chunky if the vegetables present are also undercooked.

After eating, the soup's flavor profile could be described in the following manner. The soup's aroma was just about right, but the soup initially tasted much too salty. Bitterness or sourness was not detected and the sweetness was much too low. The broth's savoriness was also somewhat subdued and its texture was much too watery. Overall, the soup was disliked very much. This profile description describes a flavor experience that incorporates the components of aroma, taste, and texture.

Adjusting Flavor Outcomes

Since taste and flavor are two sides of the same coin, adjusting a recipe's taste changes its flavor profile. These adjustments can be quantitative in nature, such as adding more of an ingredient. Adding more salt to a recipe increases its saltiness.

Beyond these simple changes, tastes can be paired to bring recipe flavors into balance or produce flavor outcomes that alone each could not achieve. These flavor pairings are useful in adjusting recipe outcomes or as quick fixes when small adjustments are required. People who do not like bitter tastes can avoid eating bitter-tasting foods, such as bitter greens or some vegetables.

Another way to manage the bitterness in food is with the use of salt. Saltiness subdues bitterness. In traditional forms of Japanese pickled vegetables where no vinegar is used, salt suppresses the bitterness in vegetables like radishes. Bitterness is also balanced by sweetness and harmonizes well with foods that have a high fat content.

The bitterness of watercress in salads can be balanced by the addition of sweet Vidalia onions and Gala apples. The addition of avocadoes, with their high fat content, could also complement the watercress with their creamy, rich taste.

Many people add cream or whole milk to their daily coffee to balance its bitterness. The fat in the cream coats the tongue and helps reduce the coffee's bitterness. Salt also pairs well with sweetness as experienced in salted caramel, trail mixes that include M & M candies or even chocolate-covered potato chips. Salt and umami have a positive synergy when paired, enhancing each other more than when used alone. Bacon-wrapped cocktail sausages and chicken soup with bacon are examples.

Sourness is offset by the addition of fat. Classic oil and vinegar-based dressings are good examples. Similarly, Tzatziki sauce, served with gyros sandwiches, is made with sour-tasting vinegar or lemon juice. These tastes are counterbalanced by the addition of yogurt (fat) that rounds out their sourness and acidity.

On the other hand, fattiness is a problem in some sauces that is resolved by the addition of vinegar that cuts the oiliness of the sauce and brightens its flavor. Sourness and saltiness also work together well in pickled vegetables that use vinegar as a preservative.

Sweet tastes are also balanced by sourness. Lemonade is a classic example where the sourness of lemons is balanced by the sweetness of sugar. The sourness of tomatoes or unripened store-bought strawberries can be brought into balance by the addition of sugar. Sweetness and fattiness seem to be made for each other in the form of pastries, cakes, and other baked goods.

Umami, the fifth taste, pairs well with other foods that also contain umami. The cheeseburger on the menus of fast food restaurants is a classic example. The grilled or browned beef has that meaty umami flavor, complemented by the cheddar cheese that contains naturally occurring glutamic acid (umami). Another classic lunch combination is grilled cheese served with tomato soup. These foods provide an umami-rich experience that comes from both the cheese and the tomatoes in the soup.

Umami in foods like these is experienced daily by people as much as any other taste components. These flavor relationships are summarized in Appendix II and common ingredients are sorted by their taste profile in Appendix III. These two appendices used together aid in adjusting flavor outcomes.

Flavor pairings applied in the form of quick fixes can help correct for tastes that differ from person to person and also for small recipe errors. Since saltiness is balanced by sourness, adding a little too much salt can be balanced with something sour, like a squeeze of lemon or lime juice.

On the other hand, if something is bland-tasting, an easy fix is to add some salt unless the ingredient flavor is substantially lacking. Adding more salt to a flavorless dish only makes the outcome salty-tasting. When too much salt is added, there is not a quick fix, but a second batch can be made and the two quantities combined together.

For soups, there is the possibility of adding a fat, like milk or cream that dilutes the salt concentration and at the same time provides a silky mouthfeel. If a recipe just needs to be brightened or a spark added, try adding an acid like vinegar or adding an aromatic at the end of cooking. Adding something spicy in the form of pepper could be a simple adjustment to help make something more distinctive.

Refreshing a recipe with a small amount of alcohol that was also used in the recipe during its development can brighten a dish just before serving. When food is too spicy, adding more of the other recipe ingredients can temper the heat. If appropriate, try diluting the recipe with milk or cream instead of water. The fats in these liquids will bind with the spicy oils (Hemphill, 2002).

Recipes that taste a bit sour can be adjusted by adding a touch of sweetness. Conversely, something too sweet can be balanced with something sour or a spice can be added. Aromas can be rekindled by simply reheating an item briefly. Warming bread rolls, pie slices, or even tortilla chips in the oven releases some of their aromas and improves their flavor.

Liquids that are too watery can sometimes be reduced (evaporated) to concentrate their flavors and also thicken their consistency. Reducing sauces naturally thickens their consistency and provides a smooth mouthfeel. Quicker thickening methods include using a mixture of cornstarch and water (slurry) or heating a mixture of a fat and flour to make a roux.

Adjusting flavor outcomes does not have to involve the addition of ingredients or changes in ingredient quantities. Simply using a different form of the same ingredient can enhance flavor without changing ingredient relationships. In baking and pastries, an expensive Madagascar bourbon vanilla can replace a store house brand. This change may or may not be noticed, however, depending on the vanilla's role in the recipe. In vanilla crepes where vanilla is a key flavor, the change will likely be more noticeable.

Regarding fresh vegetables, tomato types are rarely differentiated in stores or farmers' markets. Bins are simply labeled vine ripened, hothouse grown, heirloom, or just tomatoes. Some market vendors do not even know what variety they are selling. The varieties available in farmers' markets may be the same ones sold wholesale to stores that are developed for transportability and not necessarily their flavor. Descriptions in seed catalogs and sampling reveal a variety of tomato flavor differences. Tomatoes can be described as acidic, smoky, sweet-tasting, or even citrusy tart-flavored (Totally Tomatoes, 2014).

These differences are more apparent in leafy salads from the contrasting flavors tomatoes provide. For the average consumer, the only way to get varietal flavors is to grow them or have access to people who grow their own food.

Since flavor is more than just taste, care needs to be taken when substituting ingredients based on their taste alone. Saltiness in recipes can come from salt addition or the use of ingredients that contain large quantities of sodium. Salty-tasting ingredients include soy sauce, fish sauce, and soybean miso.

These three ingredients are not equally interchangeable with salt for several reasons. Soy and fish sauces are liquids and miso comes in paste form. Texturally different, the sodium content in one tablespoon of each ingredient is also not the same. Table salt contains 6,976 milligrams/18 grams (one tablespoon). Using the same volume measure, soy sauce contains 879 milligrams/16 grams, fish sauce contains 1,413 milligrams/18 grams, and miso 634 milligrams/17 grams (Agricultural Research Service, 2013). The latter three ingredients contain a lot of sodium, but nowhere near as much as table salt in the same amount.

The ingredients also differ in their aroma. Salt does not have a smell whereas soy sauce's aroma can be described as sweet or sour, depending on whether its brewed or not (Kikkoman, 2014). Fish sauce has a smell that comes from fermented anchovies.

The color of the ingredients in their raw state differs when diluted in a clear liquid like water. Table salt is white-colored when dry and when mixed in water it dissolves clearly. Soy and fish sauces are reddish-brown and turn water a brownish color. Miso comes in different forms but generally ranges from light brown to reddish. Mixed with water, miso turns the solution its color profile. Outside of these flavor considerations, soy sauce, fish sauce, and miso are mainly used in Asian cuisine whereas salt is used across the world.

These differences, however may, be exactly what are needed to enhance the flavor of a dish that requires saltiness. Homemade turkey gravy made from turkey drippings is seasoned with salt and pepper like many other sauces. Using soy sauce to season the gravy instead of kosher or table salt enhances the flavor in ways that salt alone cannot.

The color of gravy comes from the pan drippings that have browned on the pan bottom. This source of flavoring and coloring may not be sufficient to achieve the rich-looking gravy that people expect. Soy sauce's dark color may be just what is needed to enhance the visual appearance of the sauce. Soy sauce is high in umami, creating a classic pairing of umami and another source of umami derived from the turkey juices. The flavor of the soy sauce in small amounts adds depth to the gravy's profile, rather than just saltiness.

Before making a conscious decision to use soy sauce in turkey gravy, first consider its differences from salt and then, if considered advantageous, try it as a salt substitute or addition.

Besides these flavor considerations, ingredients may exhibit different cooking properties that need to be considered before substitution takes place. These divergent properties may not only affect flavor but may also have secondary effects as well.

Honey can be substituted for granular sugar in some baking recipes, but it also attracts and holds onto moisture from the air due to its hygroscopic nature (Amendola & Rees, 2003). Sugar also holds moisture but not to as great an extent as honey.

Attracting moisture from the air in a baked good may be a desirable quality. On the other hand, using honey without thought to its properties may yield an undesirable result.

Forgoing the use of table sugar in favor of honey also applies to the development of hot foods where appropriate. The sweetness of sugar and honey is not the same and needs to be factored in when substitutions are made. Refined sugars can also be omitted and replaced with the flavor of caramelized sugars that form naturally through a sauté of onions, carrots, or roasted red bell peppers. Adding carrots to marinara sauce is one way to add some sweetness to balance the sourness of the tomatoes without adding table sugar.

Flavor Layering in Recipes

Adjusting flavors near the end of cooking is one way to bring recipe flavors into balance. Quick fixes make adjustments just before the food is served. Adjusting flavors before cooking begins is a second method that incorporates pairing concepts and ingredient substitution.

Flavor layering is a third method that builds flavors throughout the recipe's development, not just up front or near the end. Complementary ingredients, methods, and techniques are introduced throughout the recipe's development. The outcome is like a layered cake that is more flavorful than any one of its individual layers. Recipes that use layering have an extended flavor profile experience.

The s'more, a dessert made of chocolate, toasted marshmallows, and graham crackers, is a good example. Overall, the bitter undertones of high quality chocolate are complimented by the sweet tastes of caramel and the marshmallows themselves. Roasting the marshmallows adds another layer of flavor and enhances the dessert's visual appeal. The initial crunchy texture of the graham crackers is followed by the creamy caramel and soft interior of the marshmallow. When eaten together, a whiff of steam coming out of the marshmallow carries the aromas of the chocolate and graham crackers into the nose.

Layered together, recipe ingredients and techniques create a depth of flavor that a single ingredient alone could not accomplish. When reviewing recipes, consider how flavor is developed throughout the recipe. Are the flavors developed all at the same time, like adding a package of taco mix to ground beef? Do ingredients and techniques work together in the recipe to improve taste and add flavor complexity?

Flavor layering is also used in the development of hot foods, where even small changes can enhance flavor complexity. Basic techniques can be used to layer flavors using existing recipe components. Layering does not have to include the addition of new or substituted ingredients.

Coriander and cumin seeds can be toasted first, ground, and then added to a barbeque spice mix. Toasting spices in a dry pan makes use of equipment that is already on hand and does not take a lot of additional time to execute.

Layering strategies also consider the order in which ingredients are added. Marinara sauces typically add fresh basil off of the heat just before service. This late addition provides an intense flavor boost to the sauce. Adding the basil earlier allows its flavors to be incorporated instead of added "on top" of the finished sauce. Adding fresh basil when recipe onions and garlic are sweated allows its flavors to incorporate during the sauce's development. If additional flavor intensity is wanted, the basil can be added again just before the sauce is served.

The same layering strategy can be applied to the use of salt that is typically added all at once in recipes. Salt added over several additions takes into consideration the sodium contributed naturally from other recipe ingredients. Layering in spices over several additions also allows for their integration and refreshment as the recipe develops. Incorporating a basic technique or changing the timing of ingredient additions are also ways to layer in flavor, making use of existing ingredients.

Moving on to more ambitious layering strategies, ingredient substitution

---

Recipe 3-1

Seasoned Lentils

Ingredients

lentils, dried
bay leaf
garlic clove
salt
water

Directions

Bring water to a boil and add lentils. Reduce heat to a simmer and add remaining ingredients. Cook until the lentils are tender and serve.

---

can improve overall flavor depth. Using a flavored liquid instead of water is one such layered approach. Homemade stocks made without the addition of MSG have that natural umami taste.

In a recipe for chili that calls for water, using chicken or beef stock can improve the overall flavor. Using chicken stock (for milder tastes) or beef stock (for stronger flavors) adds complexity and depth and meets the liquid requirement of the recipe. Stock can also be used to remove the browned bits stuck to the pan bottom (deglazing). Substituting wine or stock adds another layer of flavor. Layering with liquids even extends to steaming where water is normally used. Fruit juices add their own flavors through the release of their aromatic volatiles during evaporation.

Fully layered recipes go beyond ingredient substitution and build flavors that support each other throughout the recipe's development. Recipes that contain these traits may have to be created and are not found through simple Internet searches.

The process can end up being complex, but it initially begins with a basic recipe. Flavor layers are added in the form of ingredients and techniques that go together well. Seasoned Lentils (Recipe 3-1) can be prepared by simmering them in water with some salt, a garlic clove, and a bay leaf. Boiling and simmering transforms hard, dry lentils into tender ones. Water does not add flavor to the legumes, but it takes up the flavors of the other ingredients that are then absorbed during cooking. Any remaining liquid serves as a sauce.

From this simple beginning, adjustments are made to recipe ingredients and additional methods are added. Starting with five ingredients and two cooking methods, the recipe can take many directions. Bay leaves and garlic are good selections to flavor the lentils, but they represent ingredient choices more than a flavor direction.

The decision to work with Middle Eastern flavors (Recipe 3-2) ties ingredient choices to a region of the world. Middle Eastern flavors are subject to some interpretation but probably eliminate the use of coconut, pineapple, and soy sauce that are ingredients from other parts of the world. The first flavor layer added is sweetness in the form of caramelized onions to counterbalance the bitterness of the original recipe's garlic. The sauté method caramelizes the sugars in the onion, rendering them sweeter in taste. Blended oil facilitates high-temperature browning and adds flavor of its own. Since fats help to balance bitterness, their addition to the recipe helps balance the taste of the garlic.

Boiling and simmering the lentils in vegetable stock tenderizes the dried legumes and develops the second layer of recipe flavor. Unlike water, the

---

Recipe 3-2

Seasoned Middle Eastern Lentils

Ingredients

lentils, dried	vegetable stock
olive and canola oil blend	salt and Pepper
onion, chopped	
garlic cloves, minced	
cumin, ground	
cinnamon, ground	
allspice, ground	

Directions

Heat oil in a sauté pan over medium high heat. Sauté the onion until lightly browned and softened. Add the garlic and cook until fragrant. Add the spices and mix through. Add the stock and lentils; bring to a boil. Reduce heat to medium-low and simmer until done.

Recipe 3-3

Middle Eastern Lentils in Wine Sauce

Ingredients

olive oil and bacon - brunoise
carrots, celery, onions - brunoise
thyme, cumin, coriander, cinnamon
white wine and chicken stock
lentils, dried
salt and pepper
vinegar and sugar

white and sherry wines
rosemary and thyme - minced
onion - small diced
Granny Smith apple - small diced
caraway seeds, peppercorns, rosemary
brown stock

Directions

Sweat bacon in a sauté pan along with a small amount of olive oil. Add carrots, onions, celery; cover the pan and sweat until softened. Add fresh thyme and part of the spice mix. Deglaze the pan with white wine; add stock, lentils, salt, pepper, and the remaining spice mix. Cook until the lentils are done and have absorbed the liquid. Add salt and pepper, sugar and vinegar off heat. In a small pan, add white wine, sherry, herbs, spices, and brown stock. Simmer, reduce, strain, and add to cooked lentils.

---

vegetable stock imparts its own earthy flavors and adds an umami taste from the mushrooms used in the stock's development. The Middle Eastern spices are a balance of bitter and sweet tastes. Cumin is bitter but is counterbalanced by the sweet tastes of cinnamon and allspice. The spice addition represents a third layer added on to the original recipe. This new version is more layered than the original and flavor development can stop here.

This second recipe, however, still has flavor options to be explored when its ingredients and methods are reconsidered. Caramelized onions and garlic taste great but are also strong flavors at the same time. What if a more subtle approach were taken to flavor development that did not use the high heat of a sauté or the strong flavor of garlic? Removed from the recipe, garlic's bitterness does not need to be balanced by the sweetness of caramelized onions.

This change in direction opens up new possibilities for flavor development (Recipe 3-3). Traditional aromatics (*mirepoix*) can replace the stronger flavors of sautéed onions and garlic. The aromatics are cut into one-eighth inch cubes (*brunoise*). Small in size, they release their flavors quickly and texturally recede into the recipe background, being about the same size as the lentils (Figure 3-2). The bacon is also cut into one-eighth inch cubes and adds smokiness and saltiness to the recipe.

Cooking the bacon increases the total volume of oil in the pan to sweat the aromatics. Blended oil is not needed since high-heat temperatures are not used. Bacon fat provides a counterbalance to the flavor of the olive oil. The lower heat of a sweat maintains the bacon's tenderness that would otherwise become hard and crunchy from the high heat of a sauté.

Herbs and spices are added next. Fresh thyme and cumin are bitter while coriander and cinnamon are sweet-tasting, creating a balanced blend. Not all of the spices are added at one time, allowing their flavors to develop initially and then be refreshed later in the cooking process. Deglazing the pan with

Figure 3-2 A *brunoise* knife cut creates in an eighth inch carrot cube whose size is about the same as the lentils. As a result, the carrots do not texturally complete with the lentils.

wine stops the sweating process and incorporates all the flavors created in the pan. There are no residual browned bits on the pan bottom since the ingredients were sweated and not sautéed or browned. Chicken stock is added, along with the lentils and the remaining dry spice mix. The first addition of salt and pepper is made at this time.

The lentils are added and cooked until the surrounding liquid has been absorbed. This technique infuses the lentils with all the liquids' flavors so nothing is lost. A small amount of vinegar is added off-heat to brighten the lentil flavor, counterbalanced with a little bit of sugar. Vinegar is added after the lentil cooking has finished. Added earlier, the vinegar would toughen the lentils. Salt and pepper are introduced a second time, based upon a sample tasting of the cooked lentils.

In many lentil recipes, the cooking liquid also serves as the sauce, but in this recipe the cooking liquid is used to flavor the lentils and has all been absorbed. Making a separate sauce is an opportunity to add a final and fresh layer of flavor to the recipe. Layers that are added last are often tasted first since they are not as well incorporated through long cooking.

The sauce uses some of the same ingredients that were used earlier in the cooking process, providing flavor continuity. White wine, thyme, onion, and pepper are in both the lentil cooking liquid and in the sauce. The use of rosemary and caraway seeds complements the thyme flavors. Granny Smith apples add a touch of sweetness and the flavor of fresh fruit. Brown stock adds a rich flavor developed from the use of roasted bones, caramelized vegetables and hours of simmering.

The sauce is reduced and strained, removing any physical hints of the ingredients used in its flavor development. Biting into a peppercorn or rosemary leaf is not a good flavor experience. Seasonings can be adjusted again at this point to make sure the saltiness is in balance. The resulting thickened sauce is smooth in texture, coating the tongue and adding richness to the tender lentils.

This final version of the recipe is the most complex and demanding of a person's skill and knowledge. The recipe also takes more time to prepare. Additional ingredients have been added during the recipe's development to help in flavor development. The layered result provides the flavor complexity that unfolds through a longer flavor experience. In the end, ingredients, methods, and techniques have been layered on top of one another to result in a flavorful profile.

Ingredient Pairing

Peas and carrots are two ingredients that just seem to go together well. Common use in recipes makes their association easily recognizable. Established ingredient pairings are useful in flavor development since they save time trying to match flavors.

In most cases, an ingredient will be highly associated with just a few ingredients but works well with many others. Peas also go well with butter, mint, and basil. These affiliations are so strong in some cases that the resulting group describes a type of cuisine. Cayenne pepper, crayfish, and Chilies are common ingredients in Cajun cuisine where they form a strong association with one another (Page & Dornenburg, 2008). The use of crayfish and cayenne pepper seems out of place in German cuisine for this reason.

Sometimes ingredients make up a cuisine as well as define their country of origin. Japanese cuisine describes a grouping of ingredients and is the name of the country of origin. On the other hand, Middle Eastern cuisine refers to a region and not a particular country like Turkey or Saudi Arabia. Finding ingredients that are specific to only one country may be difficult. Over time, local, regional, and national cuisines integrate through foreign invasion, cooperative efforts, or the resetting of political boundaries. As a result, cuisines overlap and share ingredients from what would otherwise be two different countries.

Pickled plums (*umeboshi*) common in Japan come from the ume tree (*Prunus mume*) that actually has its origin in China (Dirr, 1990). Finding a source that describes cuisines from around the world and their influences is not a simple task. One good source is *International Cuisine* by Chef Jeremy MacVeigh (2009) that provides food histories that run the gamut from continents to islands.

Ingredient associations are increasingly becoming more inclusive as flavors are integrated between countries. Chef Ming Tsai, who promotes east-meets-west recipes on his television show and in his books, is one example.

Increasingly, large ingredient groupings are necessary to describe ingredient affinities instead of simple pairings that go together well. An excellent resource, perhaps one of the few dedicated to identifying these groupings, is *The Flavor* Bible by Karen Page and Andrew Dorneberg (2008). Their book contains charts of matching flavors based on the input of chefs, restaurant menus, websites, and cookbooks. The charts of matching flavors are quite extensive. Eggplant alone has eighty-one matching flavors. Even Thai basil has fourteen flavor matches. With so many choices, at some point everything appears to work with everything else. Page and Dorneberg identify flavor affinities and highly recommended pairings, but in many ways the charts are a more of a guide than a solution for a particular situation.

Kris Brower, in his book *Ingredient Pairings, a Cooking Reference of Complementary Ingredients* (2011), also identifies groups of associated ingredients. Using a computer program, Brower compiled just under one million recipes that were publically available on the Internet. Unlike in Page and Dorneberg's work, ingredient associations are not based on their flavor affinity. Instead, the number of times ingredients are found together is measured.

Ginger and allspice work together to flavor ginger cookies, but also may include baking soda to cause them to rise. Baking soda, ginger, and allspice are not matching flavors, but their use together in many recipes links them together statistically. Although correlated strongly, their use together does not suggest that their flavors are complementary.

Of interest in Brower's book, however, is the listing of products like 7-Up (the carbonated beverage) that pairs strongly with Jell-O brand gelatin and Kool-Aid. The matching of commercially made products is an aspect that Page and Dorneberg's work does not address.

Books on flavor matching are great culinary assets, but their information works best when considered within a recipe's context. Eggplant and olive oil complement each other when used in sautés, grilled over a fire, or roasted in an oven, but they do not work together deep-fried because of olive oil's lower smoke point.

The cooking method is also a consideration when pairing flavors. Flavor matching becomes more complicated when cuisine types are mixed together. Creativity sometimes justifies an approach where anything goes as long as the ingredient has a purpose. Tabasco sauce in a Japanese cucumber salad is sometimes added to increase its piquancy but is not representative of traditional flavors. Tabasco has its origin in Avery Island, Louisiana, a far distance from Japan. Adding hot sauce changes the salad's flavor profile that traditionally would be sweet, sour, and salty.

First and second-generation Japanese-American salads favor a sweeter taste (Nisei, 1967) but do not include ingredients that introduce spiciness.

Pairing is more than identifying ingredients that could work together. Ingredients must make sense in the context of the recipe. Recipes that are represented as traditional forms but significantly alter their flavor profiles do not represent their classic flavor combinations well.

Ingredients have different roles in recipes. Some ingredients work to support flavor development, while others are meant to make stronger flavor statements. In general, beef pairs well with an array of vegetables that include mushrooms, carrots, celery, and shallots. Recipes for sautéed beef may include some of these ingredients, but stronger flavor statements are made with some of these ingredients over the others. Mushrooms are widely used in beef sautés. Carrots, on the other hand, could be used as a supporting component but not as the primary flavoring ingredient along with the beef.

Books containing matching flavors are good reference materials, but their wide-ranging suggestions need to be considered within the context of the recipe and its intent.

Preserving Natural Flavors

Flavor preferences change over long periods of time. In the seventeenth and eighteenth centuries, plain vanilla ice cream was the most prevalent flavor (Olver, 2014). With advances in technology, confetti cake and French silk pie are just a few of the choices available today at Dairy Queen franchises (Dairy Queen, 2014).

On the other hand, flavors from the past are sometimes preferred over newer ones. Heirloom tomatoes are sought after over modern day selections because of their old-time flavor. At an even earlier point in culinary history, native food species produced the flavors that people enjoyed and consumed on a regular basis. In urban cities, these woodland, wetland, and prairie areas to mention a few places have largely disappeared.

The need for more housing, businesses, and transportation facilities has transformed large continuous tracts of natural lands into highly disturbed and fragmented areas (Williams, Schwartz & Vesk et al., 2009). Native food species are left to survive on these small, fragmented parcels of land, their conservation being an outgrowth of the larger need to preserve the beauty of nature or state and federally named endangered species. Land use changes have been necessary to meet the needs of a growing population but have caused the loss of many species, including those that are sources of food.

Today, our affinity for natural flavors has been replaced by foods that come picked, packaged, and organized into convenient grocery store displays. For those with access to specialty stores, food is artfully arranged to make the whole experience more appealing and enticing.

Unfortunately, some urban communities have little or no access to grocery stores that offer fresh foods. The flavor palate in these food deserts is limited to fast food restaurants and convenience store purchases. For people who do not cook regularly, ready-to-eat foods can be purchased at stores and membership warehouses where the ingredients may not even be listed.

People who have access and time can make a trip to a farmers' market that brings fresher flavors to the table. Taking more of a commitment, community supported agriculture (CSA) is an increasingly popular way of buying local and seasonally fresh food directly from a farmer (Schnell, 2007). Food from these two sources, however, develops people's preferences for cultivated fruits and vegetables and not their wild forms. These natural flavors are abandoned.

Many people consider cultivated forms of vegetables and fruits natural if they are grown organically and are not genetically modified. Cultivated food species grown in agricultural plots do not have the same relationship to the land as food species grown in nature. These altered relationships suggest that cultivated forms are not wholly natural but have been altered by humans and not through natural selection. These horticultural methods may improve the transportability, visual appearance, or arguably the taste of a species, but they do not represent the original taste experience.

Plants naturally live in communities, develop associations, and share common resources (Barbour, Burk, & Pitts, 1987). These wild places do not resemble commercial farms but are more like human communities where diverse inhabitants live in association with each other and share common resources. Plant communities are named just like human communities, have a shared historical heritage, and make use of the resources around them.

Plant communities interact with the land in much the same way people do, putting the needs of nature in competition with those of humans. The result is that nature and human needs often collide. On the other hand, with these commonalities, are urban cities natural communities? Cities can be described as "Neither wholly natural nor wholly contrived. It is not 'unnatural' but rather

Figure 3-3 Juneberry (*Amelanchier canadensis*) in the urban landscape, surrounded by turf grass and planted with blue colored grape hyacinths. Juneberry has showy white flowers in the spring and edible berries in June that often go unused.

a transformation of 'wild' nature by humankind to serve its own needs. . . ." (Spirn, 1984).

In urban cities built of concrete and stone, people need to be reminded of the natural world that once existed around them. Some food plants remind you of nature's beauty when they are used in urban landscapes. Unfortunately, their food value is largely ignored. The juneberry (*Amelanchier canadensis*) is a common ornamental tree used for its spring white flower show and orange-red fall color. Residential landscapes, shopping malls, and housing subdivisions incorporate this species for its ornamental characteristics. Surrounded by lawn, decorative mulch, and grown with other non-native species (Figure 3-3), its relationship with the land has been altered to meet the needs of people.

Although mostly absent from the urban environment, natural relationships continue to function for some food species where land has been preserved for future generations. Visiting these places reconnects people with the complexities of nature and demonstrates what is missing in our everyday flavor experience.

Figure 3-4 Water in a woodland? Seasonal ponds of water are found in this Flatwoods community, enriching its biodiversity that also includes wild strawberry.

Wild strawberry (*Fragaria virginiana*) is found in one of these natural woodland communities about thirty miles north of downtown Chicago in the suburb of Glencoe, llinois. Located at the Chicago Botanic Garden, Mary Mix McDonald Woods is a native oak woodland about forty hectares in size. Open to the public, the woodland actively supports scientific, educational, and visitor programs for the purpose of preservation, study, and teaching.

McDonald Woods was farmed and logged during its history, but through active management its natural communities are being restored and preserved for future generations. Wild strawberry can be found in the Flatwoods community that forms the entrance to the woodland. As its name implies, this community occurs on level or nearly level ground.

The community also is characterized by the presence of an underlying ground layer that inhibits the flow of groundwater (The Chicago Wilderness Consortium, 2006). This condition allows low-lying areas in the landscape to function as seasonal ponds (Figure 3-4). Although these temporary ponds contain no fish, they support a diverse array of aquatic invertebrates and a variety of plants that can withstand both seasonally wet and dry conditions.

Figure 3-5 Wild strawberry (shown centered) found with wild geranium (*Geranium maculatum*, upper left corner), and orange jewelweed (*Impatiens capensis*, center right).

Woodlands like the Flatwoods community contain more than just trees and are places that wild strawberry can be found.

Strawberries are about two inches in size and bright red on grocery store shelves. Their large size and bright color should make them an easy find against the green colors of other woodland species. In their natural and not cultivated form, wild strawberry fruits are actually much smaller in size and are oval in shape (Peterson, 1968).

Consistent with many perennials, the strawberry's fruits and flowers do not remain visible for extended periods of time. Unless the timing is right, no fruits will be present for identification. If the berries are not present, the leaf shape and color may be two of the identifying traits left to facilitate location of the species.

Fortunately, wild strawberries do not live alone but grow alongside other plants in the Flatwoods community. Locate the associated species and wild strawberries might also be found. Instead of looking for a single plant, the search broadens to a larger group of known associates. Some of these affiliated species (Figure 3-5) include wild geranium (*Geranium maculatum*) and orange jewelweed (*Impatiens capensis*).

At least three vertical layers make up the community structure. There are trees that make up the canopy layer, shrubs in the understory, and the plants in the ground layer. Wild strawberry is found in the ground layer. As people look towards the horizon instead of down at their feet (Figure 3-6), wild strawberry can get lost in the mix.

The green mass in the image foreground is actually made up of many species. Wild strawberry (*Fragaria virginiana*) is located along the bottom edge of the image (1) and a short distance into the picture (2). The fine-textured plant (3) that looks like lawn grass in the lower right corner of the image is wild onion (*Allium canadense*).

The wider-bladed grass-like species (4) mixed in with the wild onion is woodland brome (*Bromus pubescens*). Orange jewelweed (*Impatiens capensis*) grows close to the ground near the bottom of the image (5). The whorled leaved species with its fuchsia colored flowers (6) is wild geranium (*Geranium maculatum*).

Enchanter's nightshade (*Circaea quadrisulcata canadensis*) has leaves that come to a point like an arrowhead (7) and is found near the lower left corner of the image. Poisonous plants like nightshade are part of the community as well. Not everything is a source of food, so caution is always necessary.

Tall goldenrod (*Solidago altissima*) acts as a dark green backdrop (8) to the foreground species. The tree with a large trunk (9) in the upper left quadrant of the image is one of the Flatwood community's dominant trees, swamp white oak (*Quercus bicolor*).

At the base of this tree (10) is American hazelnut (*Corylus americana*), a shrub in the understory. As the season continues into summer and fall, some of these plants will grow taller, flowers will fade away, and others will take their places in an ever-changing display of texture and color.

The Flatwoods is only one community type where wild strawberry can be found growing. Plants, like people, can live in different communities. Some species can only live in a narrow range of places, which is why some are endangered or threatened as their specific habitat type is destroyed or adversely affected. Wild strawberry is not one of these species and is more widely found.

According to Swink and Wilhelm (1979), one of these communities is the prairie where wild strawberry associates with sky-blue aster (*Aster azureus*), false toadflax (*Comandra richardsiana*), horsetail (*Equisetum arvense*), and

Figure 3-6 Wild strawberry in the context of its broader Flatwoods community includes trees, shrubs and other species in the ground layer. Wild strawberry is located along the bottom edge of the image just left of center (1) and again about a meter away (2).

prairie phlox (*Phlox pilosa*), among others. In grassy fields, wild strawberry can be found with yarrow (*Achillea millefolium*), Canada blue grass (*Poa compressa*), common cinquefoil (*Potentilla simplex*), and black-eyed Susan (*Rudbeckia hirta*).

In wet, boggy habitats, wild strawberry can be found with colic root (*Aletris farinosa*), marsh shield fern (*Dryopteris thelypteris pubescens*), common boneset (*Eupatorium perfoliatum*), and royal fern (*Osmunda regalis spectablilis*), among others.

With this level of habitat adaptability, wild strawberry can be found in many places and could suggest why the species also does well as a cultivated variety in gardens or on commercial farms. Cutting or removing plants from public lands is not permitted or restricted, so enjoy getting back to the land, but please leave the species you find in their natural habitat. Preserving our flavor past is a community-based endeavor and is not about a single species alone.

What You've Been Missing in Flavor Relationships

Flavor development is the measure of good recipes. Flavor is often talked about in the context of recipe outcomes but is rarely defined. One possible reason is that food opinions are formed from seeing, smelling, tasting, touching, and hearing the foods we eat.

These influences make flavor an experience and more than an opinion of how a food tastes. Flavor is a single word, but it describes how food smells, tastes, and feels in our mouths. Sometimes a food's flavor is fully described, but many times simple statements suffice. Information is left out of recipes, and discussions on flavor are sometimes limited to the taste of the food. What is missing from these flavor discussions?

- People's perception of flavor develops from life experiences that start in childhood. Flavor preferences can remain the same over time or change when adulthood is reached.

- Tasting is done in people's mouths that can distinguish saltiness, bitterness, sourness, Sweetness, and umami.

- Flavor is made up of taste, aroma, and a food's texture.

- Salt comes in different forms and is used for a variety of culinary purposes. Some fresh foods naturally contain a lot of sodium without the addition of salt.

- Bitterness is a taste that people readily identify but can be confused with sourness since some foods are both bitter and sour at the same time.

- Sour-tasting ingredients can brighten up the flavor of foods because of the contrast they provide.

- Sweetness often comes in the form of refined sugars but also is found naturally in foods.

- Umami is considered a fifth taste that is savory in nature and a flavor enhancer. Umami occurs naturally in foods, can be formed during cooking, and comes bottled in jars.

- Aroma, or the smell of food, is important in flavor development. Without aroma, flavor would be limited to the five tastes and a food's texture.

- Mouthfeel describes the texture of food during eating. Serving temperature, spiciness, and astringency are part of the mouthfeel experience.

- Flavor profiles fully describe a food's aroma, taste, and texture.

- Taste and flavor are different but closely related. Adjusting a recipe's taste also changes its flavor profile.

- Quick fixes near the end of cooking adjust flavors right before service.

- Pairing ingredient tastes can subdue, balance, or produce flavor outcomes that each alone could not achieve.

- Ingredient substitution adjusts flavor outcomes without changing recipe quantities or adding new ingredients.

- Consider the similarities and differences between original and substituted ingredients. If possible, take advantage of differences in aroma, texture, or color to enhance the flavor of the recipe.

- Ingredients that taste similar may have different cooking properties that should be considered before substitution takes place.

- Flavor can be layered into recipes throughout their development, not just at the beginning or near the end of cooking.

- Flavor layering combines ingredients and techniques that build upon each other in recipe development.

- The result of ingredient and technique layering is an extended flavor profile experience.

- Flavor layering makes use of simple techniques or changes in the timing of ingredient additions.

- Ingredient and technique layering throughout a recipe builds deeper, complex flavors.

- Ingredients work well together from long association and use in recipes. Ingredient pairings describe a type of cuisine, define their country of origin, or both.

- Ingredient pairing works best when considered in the context of recipe techniques, flavor roles, and the recipe origin.

- Native food species once lived together in large communities with other food and non-food species.

- Native communities of food plants have largely disappeared from the urban environment and have been replaced with flavors of cultivated species.

- Natural communities can still be found in urban cities and provide a way for people to see what they are missing in their everyday food experiences.

RECIPES

Chapter Four

Recipe Design
Translating Ideas into Reality

Designing recipes is a pursuit that seems better left to professional chefs who write books or have restaurants to run. Chefs do have an incentive to create recipes, but recipe design has benefits for broader audiences as well. Design is a bridge that turns ideas into something tangible. Recipe design takes everyday ideas and turns them into recipes worth eating.

Design is a word that, unfortunately, intimidates people and sets up high expectations for outcomes, but design is not what people see. Design goes to the core of the visible and so remains hidden from view. Photographs illustrate stunning recipe outcomes that impress by virtue of their beauty and arrangement. These outcomes are what people see but are not design.

When asked to explain what design is, Steve Jobs responded by saying, "Design is how it works" (Walker, 2003) and not what things look like.

The inner workings of recipes have been explored in previous chapters, but design is needed to assemble these parts into a whole. The design process is what unravels recipe unknowns and turns them into the flavorful foods people eat every day.

Guessing is one path to unlocking these mysteries, but it leads to discoveries that may not be easily replicated. The design process offers a more systematic approach to recipe development and is not found in recipe books or magazines or discussed on cooking shows. The reason for its omission is that the process is borrowed from the field of landscape architecture that similarly deals with complex problems that need integrated solutions.

This chapter discusses the basics of the design process and applies its method to the design of a recipe for braised beef short ribs.

The Design Process

The design process involves cycles of defining problems and developing their solutions. The process is not linear and inherently faces more than one obstacle in its development. As one solution is found, another problem arises that requires attention. This cycle repeats itself until all the needs have been addressed. The design process determines what will be done, how the problem will be resolved, and how to continue the solution as long as possible into the future (Eckbo, 1969).

There are many ways to approach and solve a problem. The design process sorts through the possibilities, determines a solution, and develops ways to perpetuate the result into the future. The core framework identifies problems, gathers relevant data, develops solutions, tests answers, and evaluates results before the process begins again.

Applied to recipe design, problems focus on recipe selection and preparation. Gathering data involves researching methods, techniques, and flavor development. Solutions take the form of recipes that incorporate these data to develop flavor in foods. Testing prepares the recipe, using its ingredients, methods, and techniques. Evaluation looks at recipe outcomes and the effectiveness of the process used in development and cooking.

Traditionally, the design process is presented as a series of distinct linear steps (Simmonds, 1983) that follow in succession. In practice, design's stages swirl around in our minds (Figure 4-1), acting as entry and exit points to discovery and to the development of solutions. Researching can be done along many points in the process in the search to clarify ingredients, techniques, or methods. Evaluation often reveals a new set of problems that launches another round of the process.

In the larger picture, there is not a beginning and end since many recipes,

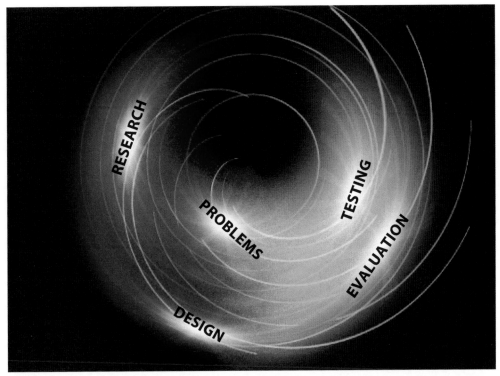

Figure 4-1 The design process involves cycles of defining problems and developing their solutions. There are five basic stages that act as points of entry and exit into the system.

techniques, and flavors evolve over time. Since design is a stage as well as the name of the process, differentiating between the two uses of the word causes confusion. People are in the design stage when many good solutions are considered but are thrown out to make something work better.

Hard choices have to be made among the many possibilities in order to produce the best solutions. These types of internal struggles are natural and experiencing these feelings places a person in the throes of design. People are in the design process when they are actively solving problems through research, design, testing, and evaluation. The design process represents the larger context where each stage has a role in defining it.

The Recipe Design Process

The design process translates well to recipe development that is also problem driven. Applied to recipes, the design process weeds out obstacles by its investigative nature. Decisions are based on close examination and the need to know more than surface information provides.

Selecting a recipe to develop is a problem many of us face. Research gathers recipes from different sources. Plenty of information already exists on the Internet and in the form of books, magazines, and television shows.

At this early stage, ignoring ingredient quantities focuses the effort on comparing ingredient types and recipe approaches. Accumulating a large number of different versions is not the goal of the process. Often there are only a few realistic or different ways that a recipe can be developed. Two or three choices form the bases of the recipe to be designed, tested, and evaluated.

At this point, things are loose and unrestrained. The "heavy lifting" of design has not yet come into play. Recipe decisions are high level in nature. Ingredient quantities are considered but not a point of focus. A brief overview of recipe directions may reveal omissions or uncover creative approaches.

The early stages of design begin with the development of recipe concepts. Researched recipe ideas have their ingredients, methods, and techniques summarized and critiqued to identify more clearly what is involved in the recipe's development.

Selected concepts have their recipe ingredients converted to the same units of measurement to be compared against one another. Design considers the results, and selects one recipe for testing. The test results and the process of development are evaluated and documented to inform future recipe decisions. The remaining part of this chapter uses the recipe design process to develop a recipe for braised short ribs in red wine sauce.

Recipe Research and Concept Development

Recipes for braised short ribs are straightforward and easy to find on the Internet and in books and magazines. With so many choices, which recipes can quickly be eliminated as concepts to develop? Read the recipe directions and confirm the cooking method. If dry-heat and moist-heat methods are not described, move onto another recipe.

Recipe techniques also influence recipe selection. Soaking short ribs in a seasoned liquid overnight (marinating) is a technique that enriches flavor but also adds an additional day to recipe development. Techniques that improve flavor but also significantly increase development time may also be used as filters in recipe selection.

Recipes for conceptual development can quickly be found on the Internet but many times the process takes longer than you might think. The same recipe is often posted under different names on multiple websites, increasing search times for unique recipes. Search engine links lead to the home page instead of to the specific recipe desired.

Links also lead to false positives where title searches point to recipes made with the correct protein but they use the wrong method. Searching for braised short ribs results in a recipe for barbequed short ribs. Personal websites and blogs contain some great ideas and recipes but are for those who already have a discerning mind for ingredients, techniques, and methods.

Initially, look for recipes that are posted on established magazine, chef, culinary author, or manufacturer's websites. Friends and family are also good sources, depending on how the recipe quantities and methods are described. When recipe choices begin to all look the same, select two or three for conceptual development.

Among the many recipe alternatives, the use of fresh herbs, Cabernet Sauvignon, and beef stock led to the selection and development of a concept for Braised Short Ribs in Red Wine Sauce (Recipe 4-1).

Dry herbs are more convenient and work well, but fresh herbs make this recipe different from the rest. Specifying Cabernet Sauvignon removed any doubt of what type of wine to use. Other recipes left the choice of wine open-ended. The use of water in some recipes is not a good choice for flavor development compared with beef stock.

Developed into a recipe concept (Concept 4-1), ingredient quantities are ignored but are grouped by their type and function. Methods and techniques are similarly listed. Summarizing the ingredients by their function, the short ribs are the protein in the recipe. Canola oil is a type of fat that is used to help brown the meat.

Salt and pepper seasonings bring out the flavor in the ribs. Aromatic vegetables add to recipe flavor. Flour is used to thicken the sauce even though the braise liquid is also reduced later through evaporation.

Tomato paste adds flavor and further research revealed that its acidity helps to break down the tough meat fibers during cooking (Anderson, 2010). Cabernet Sauvignon wine and beef stock are used as cooking liquids and create

Recipe 4-1

Braised Short Ribs in Red Wine Sauce (Yield 6 servings)

Ingredients

5 lb.	short ribs, 2" pieces
To Taste	Kosher salt and pepper
3 tbsp.	canola oil
3 med.	onions, chopped
3 med.	carrots, chopped
2 stalks	celery, chopped
3 tbsp.	all-purpose flour
1 tbsp.	tomato paste
750 ml	Cabernet Sauvignon
10 sprigs	parsley, fresh
4 sprigs	oregano, fresh
2 sprigs	rosemary, fresh
2	bay leaves, fresh
1 head	garlic
32 fl. oz.	beef stock

Directions

Preheat oven to 350 degree Fahrenheit. Season the ribs with salt and pepper. Heat the oil in a Dutch oven and brown the meat on all sides.

Set aside the ribs and reserve 3 tablespoons of the beef fat.

Add the onion, carrots and celery over medium-high heat, mix often until browned. Add flour and tomato paste and cook until a deep red color is achieved.

Add the red wine, short ribs and bring the mixture to a boil. Lower the heat and simmer the liquid until reduced by one half.

Add all the herbs and head of garlic. Stir in the stock and bring to a boil, cover and transfer to the oven. Cook the ribs 2-2 ½ hours until tender.

Strain the liquid and spoon off any fat from the surface. Preheat the broiler and pour the sauce over the meat.

Broil the ribs, turning once or twice until glazed and sizzling.

Transfer the meat onto plates, spoon the sauce on top, and serve.

Concept 4-1

Braised Short Ribs in Red Wine Sauce (Yield 6 servings)

Ingredients

Protein:	short ribs
Fat:	canola oil
Seasonings:	Kosher salt and pepper
Vegetables:	onions, carrots, celery, garlic
Thickener:	all-purpose flour
Flavoring:	tomato paste
Liquids:	Cabernet Sauvignon, beef stock
Herbs:	parsley, oregano, rosemary, bay leaves

Methods

1. Sauté
2. Boil and simmer
3. Broiling

Techniques

1. Meat browning
2. Knife chopping
3. *Pincer*
4. Deglazing
5. Reduction
6. Defatting

the moist-heat environment. There are four fresh herbs in the recipe. Referencing *The Flavor Bible* (2008), this combination generally characterizes the flavors of Italian cuisine.

The recipe directions contain several cooking methods and many techniques that work to develop braise flavor. The word sauté is not used in the directions but is suggested by the use of medium-high heat and frequent mixing and in the browned vegetable result. Boiling and simmering are the two methods that create the moist-heat cooking environment.

Broiling is a cooking method that serves an unusual function in the recipe. After several hours of braising, the ribs are ready to eat and do not require further cooking. Broiling in this instance gives the ribs a pleasing glaze.

There are six techniques in the recipe. Meat browning creates a flavorful, crusty meat exterior. The vegetables are chopped in preparation for the sauté. *Pincer* (PIN-sehr) is a French term used to describe the cooking of tomato paste to deepen its flavor. This technical term is not used, but the technique is described in the directions.

A pan deglaze is used to loosen the browned bits that are stuck to the pan bottom so that no flavor goes to waste.

Reduction is a technique used to concentrate the flavor of the braise liquids that will be further reduced during cooking in a covered environment. The reduced liquid also serves as the rib sauce before serving. Defatting the liquid keeps the amount of fat in the sauce to a minimum.

The Oven Braised Short Ribs recipe (Recipe 4-2) has its beginnings in a professional kitchen but has been scaled down for home use. Factors that point to its professional origin are yield and serving size information as well as ingredients that are weighed.

The French term *mirepoix*, used to describe the aromatics, also suggests this is not a consumer recipe. Other culinary terms include *sachet*, a French blend of aromatic ingredients tied in a cheesecloth bag. *Nappe* is a sauce consistency that coats the back of a spoon. The appeal of this recipe is its scalability and focus on technique to develop braise flavor.

The recipe's concept (Concept 4-2) is similar to the first recipe in several ways. Both recipes use short ribs, seasonings, and vegetables. Fats are used in meat browning; tomato products are used as flavorings; and wine, stock, and herbs appear again but take on slightly different forms.

The fat used in the professional recipe is a blend of olive and canola oils that add flavor and when mixed together have a higher smoke point for browning. Tomato puree is used instead of tomato paste because it has a mild flavor and a thinner consistency that allow its flavors to blend more finely.

The type of red wine is not specified since many different wines pair well for use in short rib braises. These include Zinfandel, Petite Syrah, and Shiraz/Syrah (Dornenburg & Page, 2006). Cabernet Sauvignon, used in the first recipe, is also a good choice, but it holds a more common affiliation with red meat when served as a glass of wine with dinner.

Cabernet's texture is rich and full-bodied like the meat the wine often accompanies (Simonetti-Bryan, 2010). Brown beef stock is made from roasted bones and imparts a richer flavor than beef stock (white stock) that is made

Recipe 4-2

Oven Braised Short Ribs (Yield 2.5 servings, 6 oz. serving size ~ 3 ribs)
- not including the weight of the bone

Ingredients

2 lb.	short ribs - 2.5" x 2" x 1.5" (4.5 ounce/rib)
To Taste	Kosher salt and pepper
.25 fl. oz.	canola/olive oil blend (1:1)
8 oz.	*mirepoix*
1 oz.	tomato puree
.20 oz.	garlic, sliced thick
6.5 oz.	red wine
12 oz.	brown beef stock

Sachet	
.02 oz.	thyme, dried
.05 oz.	bay leaves, dried
.01 oz.	peppercorns
.10 oz.	parsley stems

Method

Dry off excess moisture from the ribs with a towel. Trim excess fat and silverskin. Prepare and scale ingredients. Heat a 6-quart round Dutch oven over medium high heat.

Salt and pepper the ribs on both sides. Heat blended oil and brown the meat in batches. Remove the ribs, set aside and pour off the excess fat. Sauté the carrots until lightly browned. Add the onions and celery and finish browning the vegetables. Add the garlic and cook until fragrant.

Pincer the tomato puree for about a minute. Preheat an oven to 350° F. Deglaze the pan with wine. Stir and reduce the liquid until the *mirepoix* is slightly visible. Place the ribs back in the Dutch oven and add the stock, leaving the ribs partially exposed. Add the *sachet* and bring the liquid to a boil.

Seal the Dutch oven opening with foil and cover with a tight fitting lid. Place the pot in the middle of the oven for about 1.75 to 2.25 hours, turning the ribs half way through. The meat is done when a knife blade comes out cleanly. Remove the ribs and strain out the vegetables.

Defat the liquid with a separation tool and/or ladle. Use the braise liquid as a sauce or reduce to *nappe*. Serve the sauce over the ribs.

Concept 4-2

Oven Braised Short Ribs (Yield 2.5 servings, 6 oz. serving size ~ 3 ribs)
- *not including the weight of the bone*

Ingredients

Protein:	short ribs
Fat:	canola/olive oil blend
Seasonings:	Kosher salt and pepper
Vegetables:	*mirepoix*, garlic
Flavoring:	tomato puree
Liquids:	red wine, brown beef stock
Herbs/Spices:	thyme, bay leaf, and peppercorns, parsley stems

Methods

1. Sauté
2. Boil and simmer

Techniques

1. Meat fabrication
2. Vegetable small dice
3. Meat browning
4. *Pincer*
5. Deglazing
6. Reduction
7. Defatting
8. *Nappe*

---

from raw bones. The *sachet* contains mostly dried herbs and does not include rosemary or oregano.

Referencing *The Flavor Bible* (2008), this flavor combination points toward the development of French cuisine. Rosemary and oregano characterize flavors in Italian cuisine developed in the first recipe. The all-purpose flour is omitted since its use is redundant when reduction is used to create the sauce.

Boiling, simmering, and sautéing are cooking methods shared in both recipes for braised short ribs. Shared techniques include meat browning, pincer, deglazing, reduction, and defatting. Without considering ingredient quantities, the similarities in methods, techniques, and ingredients suggest that both recipes will have much the same flavor outcome.

Figure 4-2 Marbled fat that will melt away during cooking (upper left). Silverskin is a connective tissue that will not dissolve during cooking and should be removed (lower right).

Based on these commonalities alone, the flavor outcomes would be similar. Nevertheless, the outcomes are different because recipe texture is only addressed in the professional recipe for Oven Braised Short Ribs. Texture is an important component of flavor that is not specifically addressed in the consumer recipe for Braised Short Ribs in Red Wine Sauce. Short ribs come cut-to-size from local retail grocery stores but require further trimming. Meat fabrication in the recipe for Oven Braised Short Ribs not only removes excess fat but also the silverskin--a type of connective tissue that will not melt away during cooking (Figure 4-2). Eating a tough, chewy rib is not a good flavor experience. The silverskin and excess fat are left on the ribs in the other recipe.

Texture is also experienced by the way food feels in the mouth. Mouthfeel is important to a great flavor experience in recipes that have meat-based sauces. Sauce development in the Oven Braised Short Rib recipe reduces the braise liquid to *nappe* that produces a smooth, thickened sauce that coats the tongue during eating. The braise liquid is not thickened but simply strained and poured over the ribs in the other recipe. Its consistency could be watery, thick, or somewhere in between.

Glazed short ribs add to the visual experience of eating, but a watery sauce detracts from a flavorful experience. Flavor development is also affected by the way the *mirepoix* is cut in both recipes. Small-diced aromatics in the recipe for Oven Braised Short Ribs have more uniform browning that results from the suitability of all the vegetables' surface area and volume. Chopped *mirepoix* in the consumer recipe leads to random-sized vegetables that unevenly caramelize, limiting their flavor contribution in the final sauce.

Together, meat fabrication, sauce development, and technical knife cuts increase the flavor potential in the professional recipe for Oven Braised Short Ribs.

Recipe Conversion

Transitioning from conceptual development to the design stage is characterized by recipes that are refined enough where they can be compared fairly with one another. Assessing the two short rib recipes is difficult when their ingredients are measured in different units and their yields are not the same. The consumer recipe for Braised Short Ribs in Red Wine Sauce uses vegetable quantities and spoon measures and yields five pounds of ribs.

Ingredients in the professional recipe for Oven Braised Short Ribs are mostly measured by their weight and the yield of ribs braised is two pounds. To be fairly compared together, their units of measure and yield need to be the same. Converting quantities of whole vegetables to ounces is not a straightforward process. Assumptions need to be made about ingredient sizes that, unfortunately, do not have the benefit of the author's insight.

The Braised Short Ribs in Red Wine Sauce recipe specifies the use of medium carrots. Unfortunately, the size of a vegetable is a matter of personal opinion. The choice may reflect what the author had in mind or be far afield. Because it was designed for the home cook, there is a good likelihood that prepackaged carrots are used. These carrots come bundled in one-pound plastic bags and run smaller than boxed and unsorted carrots used in restaurants.

Similar decisions are required when converting the onions and celery in the recipe. Regarding the herbs, a sprig is not a standard unit of measure but a small branch or shoot of a plant. Herbs often come prepackaged and cut to length in stores. This retail size and its associated weight can be used to determine recipe amounts. The amount of wine used is equal to one bottle of wine that, rounded off, equals twenty-five fluid ounces when converted from 750 milliliters. Using the weight of water as a guide (1.041 ounces), the dry weight of the wine is twenty-six ounces. Using the same methodology, the dry weight of the beef stock is thirty-three ounces.

The remaining liquid in the recipe is the canola oil. One tablespoon equals one-half fluid ounce. The amount required in the recipe is one and a half fluid ounces of oil. The oil could be weighed as well, but the result would not be significantly different enough to affect its use to coat the pan bottom.

The first Appendix in this book provides the weight for a number of raw vegetables, fruits, and herbs and is the source of the ingredient weights in the converted recipe (Recipe 4-3). Applying the idea of baker's percentage to the development of hot foods, ingredients are expressed as a percentage of the weight of the protein that is given a value of 100 percent.

In contrast to the consumer recipe, conversion of the Oven Braised Short Ribs recipe is straightforward since its ingredients are weighed. Increasing the amount of ribs from two to five pounds represents a two-and-a-half time increase. Multiplying all the recipe ingredients by this factor maintains the same relationships that existed in the original recipe. The only ingredient not factored by the same amount is the blended oil that is rounded down to the nearest half fluid ounce. To lightly coat the pan bottom, six tenths of a fluid ounce is difficult to measure and the quantity difference does not affect the oil's function in the recipe.

The converted recipe (Recipe 4-4) shows revised ingredient amounts. The weight of each ingredient is expressed as a percentage of the weight of the short ribs that is set to 100 percent.

Recipe Design and Development

The result of recipe conversion is two short rib recipes of a comparable nature. With their output the same and their ingredients weighed, design considers flavor development in each recipe. Aromatic vegetables, herbs, wine, and beef stock are major recipe components in the Braised Short Ribs in Red Wine Sauce recipe (Recipe 4-3). The total weight of the *mirepoix* is about 53 ounces, exceeding one-half the weight of the short ribs. This amount goes beyond the

Recipe 4-3

Braised Short Ribs in Red Wine Sauce (Yield 6 servings)
Ingredients Converted to Ounces and Relative Percentages Shown.

Amount	Percent	Item
5 lb.	100%	short ribs, 2" pieces
To Taste	-------	Kosher salt and pepper
1.5 fl. oz.	2%	canola oil
2.2 lb.	44%	onions (3.5" dia. x 3"), chopped
11 oz.	14%	carrots (1.25" dia. x 8"), chopped
7 oz.	9%	celery (2.5" x 13"), chopped
.90 oz.	1%	all-purpose flour
.60 oz.	.8%	tomato paste
26 oz.	33%	Cabernet Sauvignon
1.5 oz.	2%	parsley (3" x 7"), sprig
.40 oz.	.5%	oregano (1" x 5"), sprig
.30 oz.	.4%	rosemary (1" x 6.5"), sprig
2	--------	bay leaves, fresh
3 oz.	4%	garlic head (2.5" dia. x 2")
33 oz.	42%	beef stock

Recipe 4-4

Oven Braised Short Ribs (Yield 6 servings, 6 oz. serving size ~ 3 ribs)
Ingredient Amounts Increased for the New Yield and Relative Percentages Shown.

Amount	Percent	Item
5 lb.	100%	short ribs - 2.5" x 2" x 1.5" (4.5 ounce/rib)
To Taste	-------	Kosher salt and pepper
.5 fl. oz.	.6%	canola/olive oil blend (1:1)
10 oz.	13%	onions
5 oz.	6%	carrots
5 oz.	6%	celery
2.5 oz.	3%	tomato puree
.50 oz.	.6%	garlic, smashed and sliced
16 oz.	20%	red wine
28 oz.	35%	brown beef stock
Sachet		
.05 oz.	.06%	thyme, dried
.13 oz.	.2%	bay leaves, dried
.03 oz.	.04%	peppercorns
.25 oz.	.3%	parsley stems

Figure 4-3 The herbs in the Braised Short Ribs and Red Wine Sauce recipe represent a significant flavor addition based on their ingredient quantities.

role of aromatics to one that strongly influences flavor outcomes.

Looking at the ratio between the onions, carrots, and celery, the relationships do not follow conventional practices. Using a traditional ratio, the weight of the onions should be 26 ounces. The recipe calls for 35 ounces. Based on a 2:1:1 ratio, the recipe should use about 13 ounces each of carrots and celery. Instead, the carrots weigh 11 ounces and the celery 7 ounces. Based on these quantities, the amount of onions exceeds what is necessary and dominates the flavors of the other two aromatics. The weight of the onions alone is closer to one-half of the weight of the ribs (44 percent), an appreciable amount.

The weight of the herbs may seem insignificant when compared to the *mirepoix*, but as a group they also impart strong flavors. When viewed together (Figure 4-3), they create a large bundle of herbs, not an amount whose flavor recedes into the background.

The wine is one-third the weight of the ribs before reduction, which concentrates its flavor even more. This amount indicates that Cabernet Sauvignon is another important flavor in the recipe's development.

Taken together, the *mirepoix*, herbs, and wine develop big, bold, and distinguishable flavors in the recipe. These adjectives make the recipe very appealing. On the other hand, are their flavors more important than the flavor of the beef short ribs? Do their flavors support or compete with the beef flavor that is developed through the braise method? Depending on how these questions are answered, the recipe is right on the money or needs to take a different direction. This is the point in design where good ideas may be thrown out in favor of others.

The Oven Braised Short Ribs recipe (Recipe 4-4) takes a different flavor approach and provides a good contrast to the first recipe. The cooking method may be the same, but the flavor outcome is different. The *mirepoix* is 25 percent of the short rib weight, about the same percentage used in the development of stock where the aromatics do not overshadow the flavor of the protein.

The onions, carrots, and celery are in traditional *mirepoix* ratios. The recipe onions represent about 13 percent of the rib weight, not 44 percent as reflected in the previous recipe. The amount of garlic used is .6 percent versus 4 percent of the weight of the protein--a few cloves instead of an entire garlic head.

Sixteen and not twenty-six ounces of wine are used in the development of the braise liquid. This represents about a 40 percent reduction from the quantity used in the first recipe. The amount of oil used to brown the ribs is reduced by over 50 percent in the Oven Braised Short Ribs. Although the oil coverage on the pan bottom depends on its shape and size, too much oil causes splatter. The first recipe amount does not include the contribution of the fat from the ribs during browning.

The amount of parsley used is .3 percent of the weight of the ribs compared to 2 percent used to flavor the previous recipe, a much smaller amount. Parsley stems are used instead of the whole sprig (Figure 4-4). Leaves can add bitterness to the braise liquid so they are removed. Stems without leaves are also used in stock development for the same reason. Overall, different ingredient amounts and attention to traditional ratios help bring the braise flavors into balance. Even small details like the removal of leaves from the parsley stems influence recipe flavor.

Enough information and analysis has now been completed to adjust both recipes or make a decision to use one over the other. The amount of onions in the Braised Short Ribs in Red Wine Sauce can be reduced. The remaining aromatics can be adjusted to reflect traditional *mirepoix* ratios. The amount of

Figure 4-4 Parsley stems and not sprigs with leaves are used in the cheesecloth *sachet* along with other herbs and spices. Parsley leaves can add bitterness to the braise liquid.

garlic can be changed, as well as the amount of oil, wine, or stock used. Removing the parsley leaves from their stems is an easy change to improve recipe flavor.

Changes could also be made to the Oven Braised Short Rib recipe. Increasing the quantity of *mirepoix* or garlic emphasizes their flavors. The addition of dried oregano and rosemary to the *sachet* changes its flavor profile to a more Italian bias. Ingredient weight makes these changes easier over visual guessing.

Some adjustments to both recipes are likely required in any case. Depending on the length of cooking and how well the Dutch oven is sealed, the liquid amounts of both recipes will likely have to be adjusted to meet a specific kitchen setup. The necessity of these changes will have to be evaluated during or after cooking is completed.

Techniques could also be changed in both recipes to shorten overall cooking times. The broiling method could be skipped in the first recipe and sauce development in the Oven Braised Short Rib recipe. The ribs could be plated, the braise liquid strained, defatted, poured directly over the meat, and served.

Adjustments in ingredients and techniques work together to produce a standardized recipe that produces the same result for a specific kitchen situation.

Recipe Layout

Exploring concepts, converting recipes, and making design decisions lead to recipe choices that are tested and evaluated on the basis of need. Cooking provides observable confirmation for decisions made in design. Recipes tested for the first time will likely need revision to account for specific kitchen conditions and user skills. These early versions often look like recipes people use every day. Ingredients are listed on top, followed by recipe directions. Problems are worked out through design revisions until a final recipe design is tested, approved, and documented.

Recipes for individual use can contain as little or as much information as the author wants to include. For recipes intended for other people, you may want to consider a broader group of needs that include detailed direction and scalability. Thorough explanation helps the home cook understand what is required and why. The more advanced user can glance over the detail and take advantage of ingredients that are weighed.

Design extends to the layout of recipe information and makes use of everyday commonsense principles. People in the Western world read from left to right, top to bottom. Recipe information should reflect this pattern and text should be placed accordingly. Information that is important should be placed to the left of secondary information that will be read next in order. *Chunking* is a principle that groups information together to help people find what they are looking for more quickly. Grouping ingredients into blocks of text points to their preparation together.

Long lists of recipe ingredients suggest no sense of order or sequence of preparation. *Consistency* and *repetition* are two design principles that enhance readability. Presenting information in an identifiable pattern that repeats throughout the document creates consistency. Readers benefit from knowing what to expect next. *Emphasis* conveys what the author feels is important.

Text bolding, italicizing, and changes in font size help to distinguish important information. *Balance* deals with the distribution of design elements. *Symmetry* achieves balance by distributing elements equally around the center of the page. *White space* is the area between text and objects and helps create a feeling of balance. Leaving sufficient space between blocks and lines of text lets the eye relax and take the information in a little at a time. Cramming text together may get everything on the page but will not aid readability. These basic design principles transform everyday recipes from those that inform to those that assist in the cooking process.

Recipe text can be laid out with images that reinforce or clarify major points. Pictures are helpful in most cases but are not without detractions. Large-sized images can interrupt the flow of information that describes recipe procedures. Stylized photographic images can draw attention to their artistic qualities instead of supporting recipe information. Images also have difficulty capturing taste and some aspects of food preparation. The moisture level of bread dough is discerned by feeling its texture with the hands. Digital images can only capture the outward appearance of the dough.

Pictures require the use of a camera or smart phone. Most smart phones at this time do not capture multiple still frames per second. Split second timing is helpful when capturing procedures that involve movement, such as knife cutting techniques. On the other hand, pictures in many more cases replace words and, when used well, illustrate procedures that are otherwise hard to explain. When used to support recipe text, photographs clarify recipe procedures and are welcome additions.

To this point in the chapter, the short rib recipes have their ingredients in list form and their directions as a series of paragraphs. This format is not particularly visually friendly when ingredient lists are long and directions complex.

Limiting recipe information to a single page restricts the amount of instruction that can be provided. Recipes either have their ingredients in common cup and spoon measures or are weighed in ounces for professionals. Is there a way to lay out recipes that address the needs of both consumers and professionals?

Using common design principles such as chunking, balance, consistency and a multi-page format (Recipe 4-5), recipe information is organized to meet the needs of both the home and professional cook. The single list of ingredients has been replaced with a table. Volume measures appear in the left column

Recipe 4-5

Oven Braised Short Ribs (Yield 6 servings, 6 oz. serving size ~ 3 ribs)
- not including the weight of the bone

Ingredients

Amount	Ounces	Item
18	5 lb.	short ribs -2.5" x 2" x 1.5" (4.5 ounce/rib)
TT	TT	Kosher salt and pepper
1 Tbsp.	.5 fl. oz.	canola/olive oil blend (1:1)
1 Med	10 oz.	onion (3.5" diameter x 3" high) - small diced
2 Small	5 oz.	carrot (1.25" diameter x 5.5" long) – small diced
1 ½	5 oz.	celery stalks (2.5" base x 13" long) – small diced
¼ cup	2.5 oz.	tomato puree
3	.50 oz.	garlic cloves- trimmed, smashed
16 fl. oz.	16 oz.	red wine
28 fl. oz.	28 oz.	brown beef stock

Sachet

1 ½ tsp.	.05 oz.	thyme, dried
2.5	.13 oz.	bay leaves, dried (1" wide x 2.5" long)
8	.03 oz.	peppercorns
6	.25 oz.	parsley stems (1/8" diameter x 3.75" long)

Ingredient Preparation
(Getting Everything Ready Before Cooking Begins)

Short Rib Fabrication

1. Dry off any excess moisture from the ribs with a towel and trim excess fat and silverskin (connective tissue) from the short ribs using a boning knife.

   (Wet ribs will give off steam during cooking and inhibit browning. Leave some fat for flavor development. Silverskin will not melt away during cooking.)

Vegetable Cutting

1. Peel and trim the vegetables, removing ends and leaves. Small dice the onion, carrots, and celery into one-quarter inch cubes. Peel and smash the garlic cloves with a chef knife or use a garlic press. Remove the leaves from the parsley sprigs.

(The uniform cube facilitates even browning and the small size decreases the overall cooking time. Crushing the garlic releases the oils intensifying the garlic flavor. Parsley leaves can add bitterness to the braise liquid unless soaked in cold water first.)

Sachet Assembly

1. Place the dried thyme, bay leaves, peppercorns and parsley stems in a small section of cheesecloth. Gather up the edges creating a small bundle. Tie up the cheesecloth with a section of butcher's twine long enough to attach to the handle of the Dutch oven.

(Cotton string can be substituted for twine as long as the fibers are not nylon that would melt during cooking.)

Ingredient Scaling

1. Weigh the recipe ingredients on a scale using lightweight containers. Alternatively, portion ingredients into appropriate sized containers. Make available a 6-quart round Dutch oven or heavy bottom pot with a tight fitting lid.

Cooking on the Stove Top
(Browning and Liquid Addition)

Meat Browning

1. Heat a 6-quart Dutch oven. Salt and pepper the ribs on both sides.

(Heating the Dutch over medium-high heat brings the oil to temperature faster and arguably helps keep the food from sticking to the pot bottom.)

2. Add the blended oil to coat the oven bottom and heat until hot.

(The oil will start to pool and separate, forming "legs" similar to those created by swirling wine in a glass. The oil should not heat beyond its smoke point. Adding more oil than lightly coating the pot bottom will reduce browning and increase oil splatter.)

3. Place the ribs on the pot bottom in a manner where they do not touch each other (overloading). Brown the meat on all sides, about 3-4 minutes a side. Do not cook all the ribs at one time. Instead, work in small batches. Remove the ribs and set aside. Save about one tablespoon (.5 fl. oz.) of fat and pour out the rest.

(Overloading the Dutch oven lowers its surface temperature, causing the ribs to steam rather than brown. The meat is ready to turn when the ribs release easily from the pot bottom. In between batches, some of the fat may have to be poured out to prevent

an inordinate amount of oil splatter.)

Vegetable Browning

1. **Sauté the carrots over medium-high heat for about 5- 8 minutes until browned. Add the onions and celery and continue to sauté the vegetables for about ten minutes to finish their browning.**

   (Adding all the aromatics at one time overloads the pot inhibiting caramelization of the carrots and onions. Celery contains less sugar than the other two vegetables and will not brown as well during the process. Mix the vegetables frequently, but not constantly or browning will be inhibited.)

2. **Add the garlic, mix through and cook until fragrant, about 30 seconds. Pincer the tomato puree for about one minute by working the product against the pot bottom with a spatula.**

   (Thirty seconds is just about the right amount of time to bring out the flavor of raw garlic that is characterized by its aromatic smell. Pincer concentrates the flavor of the tomato puree, lessens any canned taste and caramelizes the product a bit.)

3. **Preheat the oven to 350° F.**

Liquid Addition

1. **Deglaze the pan with wine. Lower the heat, stir and reduce down until the vegetables become slightly visible, about 10 minutes.**

   (Pour the wine in slowly simultaneously scraping the pot bottom with a heat-resistant spatula to remove any remaining browned bits (fond). Note: Most of this flavoring has already been released and absorbed by the vegetables during the sauté process. There may be little fond left to remove.)

2. **Place the ribs back in the Dutch oven and add the stock, leaving the ribs partially exposed.**

   (The level of the liquid will vary depending on the configuration of the ribs in the pot. As long as the ribs are not completely submerged below the surface of the liquid but are about two-thirds covered, the level is fine.

3. **Add the *sachet* and bring the liquid to a boil on the stove top.**

   (Find a space among the ribs to place and submerge the sachet. Tie the other end of the butcher's twine to one of the pot handles for easy removal after cooking. Bringing the braise liquid to a boil on the stovetop, distributes the heat evenly throughout the ingredients.)

4. **Enclose the top of the Dutch oven with aluminum foil and cover with a tight fitting lid.**

   (*Wrap the foil around the pot handles and pinch a seam around the rim for a better fit. Careful the rim will be hot! The foil helps keep the liquid from evaporating too quickly over the long cooking time.*)

Cooking in the Oven
(*Moist-Heat Cooking*)

Short Rib Tenderizing

1. **Place the Dutch oven in the middle of the oven for about 1.75 to 2.25 hours, turning the ribs halfway through. Add more brown beef stock if the liquid level falls below one-half the height of the ribs. Check the tenderness of the meat by inserting the end of a paring knife to gauge the level of resistance.**

   (*If a knife tip comes out clean and smoothly, the ribs will be tender. The meat will take on a very dark color from the wine reduction, meat browning and caramelization of vegetables.*)

2. **Remove the *sachet* and discard. Remove the ribs to a platter and cover with foil to keep warm. Strain out the vegetables and discard.**

   (*The vegetables can be pureed and used in the making of the sauce, but the liquid will not be clear.*)

Sauce Development
(*On the Stove Top*)

1. **Pour the liquid into a fat separator and wait for the layers of fat and juice to disassociate, about three minutes. Defat the liquid per manufacturer's recommendations. Alternatively, use a ladle to skim off the surface fat. Season the remaining braise liquid with salt and pepper and use as a sauce.**

   (*Typically cup and spout type separators hold some fat in their spout that gets poured out with the juices. Separators that dispense their juice from a hole in the cup bottom do not have this problem. A ladle can also be used and is a better choice than a spoon to extract small amounts of oil that reside on a liquid's surface. For small particles of fat, a paper towel can be briefly laid on top of the liquid and drawn across the surface.*)

2. **Serve the sauce over the short ribs. Alternatively, reduce the braise liquid to a *nappe* (coat the back of a spoon) consistency, season with salt and pepper, taste, adjust again, and serve over the short ribs.**

(Bring the liquid to a low boil in a saucepan and thicken naturally through evaporation. Homemade beef stock that does not congeal when cooled in the refrigerator (like Jell-O gelatin) will have difficulty thickening into a sauce through evaporation. Reduction can take twenty minutes or longer depending on the amount of liquid. To attenuate the heavy sauce texture, finish with butter (Peterson, 2008). To balance the richness and heavy mouthfeel of the sauce, add a small amount of vinegar to brighten the flavor. Canned beef broth or beef base mixed with water are better thickened with a roux.)

where most people are going to look first for information. Less commonly used scaled quantities are shown to the right. Ingredients are chunked into blocks that reflect their order of preparation together.

Additionally, ingredients are fully described to provide a clearer picture of their size and method of preparation. Instead of one long paragraph of procedures, the recipe is divided into principal operations. The process begins by getting organized and readying ingredients. Known as *mise en place* in professional kitchens, everything is in its place before cooking begins.

Ingredient preparation includes meat fabrication, vegetable cutting, *sachet* assembly, and ingredient scaling. Cooking begins on the stove top. This section includes rib and vegetable browning, a pot deglaze, and liquid addition that creates the moist-heat environment during cooking.

From the stove top, cooking takes place in the oven where the meat tenderizes and the braise liquid concentrates. Sauce development after the ribs have finished cooking produces a thickened meat sauce that goes with the ribs. Each specific task is followed by information in italics that explains why the procedure is done or includes insightful information. This pattern of task followed by explanation is used throughout the recipe, from preparation to cooking and sauce development. This designed layout provides in-depth information and describes more accurately the work necessary to complete the recipe successfully.

Incorporating photographs into the Oven Braised Short Rib recipe helps communicate the steps necessary to prepare and cook the ribs. Images can simply be inserted into the text version of the recipe. This practice is common in recipe books and websites that have a block of text followed by one or two images.

This simple approach highlights key aspects of recipe development. Perhaps four or even six images can accompany a single recipe. On the Internet, this pattern can repeat itself across many pages, introducing even more detail, but this requires a lot of scrolling. In this instance, the images are usually large in size and when correlated well with the intent of the text, provide great insight into recipe procedures.

Another approach has its roots in film photography where dozens of images are presented together in a contact print sheet, also known as a proof sheet. Strips of negatives are arranged sequentially next to each other and printed on one sheet of paper. An entire roll of film can be viewed at a single time and its images seen in the order they were taken. This idea works well for recipes whose procedures unfold sequentially from beginning to end.

This approach, however, does not allow for a great deal of text placement. Large blocks of text disrupt the flow of images and the idea is lost. The layout reverts back to blocks of text followed by a series of images. Less written instruction assumes a higher level of culinary knowledge on the part of the user. The recipe is more like a "cheat sheet" or a set of Cliff notes for recipe preparation and execution. Nevertheless, used alone, the recipe proof sheet can support more detailed text versions of the recipe. Used together, the advantages of both are put to good use.

Applied to the Oven Braised Short Rib recipe (Recipe 4-6), the proof sheet contains the same table of ingredients as the text only version but the procedures are described mainly through the use of photographs. The images are still organized by major recipe operations. Although visually different, the recipe uses some of the same design principles to organize the page.

The information is laid out to read from left to right, top to bottom. There is a consistent and repeated use of images that makeup each line of the page. Short descriptions below each picture describe the progression of steps from beginning to end.

Preparation begins with an image of silverskin removal (Photo 1) that is located at the left margin of the page. The remaining images follow to the right and down, following a natural zigzag pattern. A single image represents the dicing of vegetables and preparation of garlic, parsley stems, and *sachet* (Photo 2). The next image shows recipe ingredients scaled into appropriate-sized containers (Photo 3). This assembly of ingredients reinforces the importance of having everything ready before cooking begins.

Cooking on the stove top begins with meat seasoning (Photo 4) and heating the oil to a high temperature (Photo 5). Heated oil first pools and then

Recipe 4-6

Oven Braised Short Ribs (Yield 6 servings, 6 oz. serving size ~ 3 ribs)
- *not including the weight of the bone*

Amount	Ounces	Item
18	5 lb.	short ribs -2.5" x 2" x 1.5" (4.5 ounce/rib)
TT	TT	Kosher salt and pepper
1 Tbsp.	.5 fl. oz.	canola/olive oil blend (1:1)
1 Med	10 oz.	onion (3.5" diameter x 3" high) - small diced
2 Small	5 oz.	carrot (1.25" diameter x 5.5" long) – small diced
1 ½	5 oz.	celery stalks (2.5" base x 13" long) – small diced
¼ cup	2.5 oz.	tomato puree
3	.50 oz.	garlic cloves- trimmed, smashed
16 fl. oz.	16 oz.	red wine
28 fl. oz.	28 oz.	brown beef stock

Sachet

Amount	Ounces	Item
1 ½ tsp.	.05 oz.	thyme, dried
2.5	.13 oz.	bay leaves, dried (1" wide x 2.5" long)
8	.03 oz.	peppercorns
6	.25 oz.	parsley stems (1/8" diameter x 3.75" long)

Ingredient Preparation and Stove Top Cooking

1. Silverskin & Fat Removal

2. Vegetable Preparation

3. Scaling and Assembly

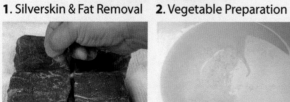
4. Season Ribs Both Sides

5. Heat the Oil

6. Place Ribs on Pot Bottom

7. Brown Ribs on All Sides   **8**. Brown Diced Carrots   **9**. Brown Celery and Onion

10. Add Garlic, Pincer Puree   **11**. Deglaze and Oven 350ºF   **12**. Stir and Reduce Down

13. Reduce Wine 50 Percent   **14**. Add Stock, Ribs, *Sachet*   **15**. Bring to Boil and Foil

16. Cook 1.75 - 2.5 Hours   **17**. Knife Test Discard *Sachet*   **18**. Strain Out Vegetables

Sauce Development on the Stove Top

19. Separate Out Fat   **20**. Clean Up with a Ladle   **21**. Serve Sauce or Reduce

separates. The image shows the oil beginning to disassociate on the pot bottom.

The next two photographs are dedicated to proper meat browning. The first image shows four short ribs placed on the pot bottom (Photo 6), making the point not to overload the pan. The second image shows the meat browned on all sides and not just on the top and bottom (Photo 7).

The next three images illustrate vegetable browning. The small-diced carrots are browned first because they take longer to develop color (Photo 8). The onions and celery are added next and a close-up shows the *mirepoix's* browned state after sautéing (Photo 9). The next image shows the *pincer* of tomato puree with a heat-resistant spatula and garlic addition (Photo 10).

Deglazing the pot bottom with wine (Photo 11) stops the browning process and helps to remove the browned bits (fond) from the pot bottom. The oven is also preheated at this time. Fond removal is aided by the use of a heat-resistant spatula (Photo 12) that scrapes the pot bottom. Moving a heat-resistant spatula through the liquid also aids the reduction process that concentrates the wine's flavor. Reduction is complete when the *mirepoix* can be seen through the liquid's surface (Photo 13).

The ribs are added back into the pot along with brown beef stock and the *sachet* (Photo 14). The level of liquid in relationship to the height of the ribs varies according to how they are stacked, however, the liquid level is below the top of the ribs. The pot is shown tightly covered with aluminum foil (Photo 15) after the liquid has been brought to a boil. The seam around the rim, described in the text-only recipe, is shown in the photograph.

Cooking in the oven is represented by a single image of the pot in the middle of an oven, tightly covered with its lid (Photo 16).

The end of cooking is represented by the insertion of a paring knife into one of the ribs to test for doneness (Photo 17). The vegetables are strained out of the braise liquid (Photo 18) before the sauce is made.

Sauce development is done on the stove top and begins with defatting the braise liquid with a fat separation tool (Photo 19). Defatting can also be done with a ladle if a separation tool is not available. Any remaining surface fat can be removed with a ladle depressed slightly into the liquid's surface (Photo 20).

There are two options for a sauce. After defatting, the liquid can be used directly or reduced to *nappe* in a saucepan. This second option is illustrated in a photograph that shows the sauce coating the back of a spoon (Photo 21). The level of liquid reduction is shown in the photograph background. The overall layout of this recipe is simple, direct, and serves as a quick reminder of what to do at each step in the recipe development. Although less written information is provided, well-chosen images convey important information that words alone have difficulty describing.

What You've Been Missing by Not Designing Recipes

Recipe design is likely the last thing on many people's minds as they look for recipes to prepare. Cooking books, magazines, and television shows place recipe design in the hands of the professional but do not guarantee success. Design is a problem-solving process whose methods can be used by many of us because they are based on common sense approaches.

Design acts as a bridge that spans the gap between problems and their solutions. Applied to recipes, the design process identifies problems before they arise and produces better outcomes. The approach advances culinary knowledge and lessens the reliance on guesswork that may lead to inconsistent results in the future.

- The design process involves cycles of defining problems and developing their solutions and is a framework borrowed from the field of landscape architecture.

- The design process identifies problems, gathers data, develops and tests solutions, and evaluates outcomes. These five stages act as entry and exit points to the process that leads to discovery and the development of solutions.

- You know you are in the middle of design when hard choices are being made that throw out good solutions in an effort to produce even better outcomes.

- The recipe design process begins by gathering recipes for a specific need. Research provides insight into ingredients, techniques, and methods that may be unfamiliar. Two or three choices are selected for development.

- Concepts summarize recipe ingredients, techniques, and methods. Ingredient quantities are ignored, but their functions are determined with the help of research.

- Concepts are compared with one another to determine differences in approach and their influence on flavor development.

- Consumer recipes are converted to dry ounces so that ingredient ratios can be determined, as well as their relative percentages.

- Design determines how ingredient quantities work together to build flavor in recipes. One recipe is selected for testing or adjustments are made to improve flavor outcomes.

- Recipes tested for the first time will likely need revision to account for specific kitchen conditions and user skill.

- Recipes that are shared should consider the needs of others. Detailed directions help those unfamiliar with the recipe's preparation. Scalability helps both consumers and professionals.

- Layout of recipe information uses common sense design principles that include reading preferences, chunking, consistency, repetition, emphasis, balance, and white space.

- Recipes can be laid out using text or text with images that document procedures and outcomes.

- Photographs help communicate difficult ideas but also need to be used with care. Images can disrupt the flow of recipe information and cannot capture some techniques, such as those involving rapid movement.

- Images laid out in a proof sheet format show recipe procedures sequentially but do not provide room for lengthy description. Proof sheets function as quick reminders of recipe procedures.

RECIPES

Chapter Five

Evaluation
Informing Future Recipe Decisions

Cooking books and television shows rarely evaluate recipe outcomes or how to assess the food preferences of others. Evaluation is addressed by the utterance of "umm, umm, good" and nothing more seems necessary.

There is not much need to assess the opinions of others since books highlight the author's recipes and cooking shows exist for the same purpose. Nevertheless, recipes come out badly and people do not always want what has been prepared.

The extent to which recipe outcomes can be generalized is limited for a number of reasons. The cook's skill, kitchen setup, interpretation of methods, techniques, and differences in equipment are just a few of the variables that cause outcomes to vary from situation to situation. Expecting recipes to come out exactly as pictured or how a chef cooks them on television is not always realistic, leaving people wondering why their dish didn't turn out right.

Expecting people to want what has been cooked is also not a given. Under these uncertain circumstances, evaluation provides information on how well an approach, product, or system is working (Frechtling, 2007), not just a judgment on success or failure. These simple up or down judgments, unfortunately, define evaluation narrowly and limit its appeal. Although meant to help, evaluation ends up with a bad reputation, is put off, and is considered not worth the effort.

Incorporated routinely as part of recipe development, evaluation leads to changes in knowledge, attitude, skills, or aspirations (Radhakrishna & Relado, 2009). Evaluation often leads to recipe adjustments that require multiple attempts to fully incorporate changes that meet an individual need.

These cooking trials improve existing skill sets and may even cultivate new competencies. Fresh insights may be gained through research that sheds new light on the problems at hand. These experiences build upon themselves and move attitudes and change perspectives that otherwise would remain unchanged over time.

There is a degree of comfort that ensues when things remain the same, but changes also bring rewards. New perspectives create avenues of exploration and open opportunities that may not have been seen in the context of old ways of thinking.

Recipe evaluation does not directly fall within traditional areas of program evaluation. A recipe is not an initiative or intervention. Nevertheless, recipe evaluation can borrow from the creative arts that use design to develop interactive products. These products may not be edible but are viewed and experienced by people everyday.

Museums use exhibits to display and interpret what they collect, preserve, and study (Neves, 2002). Museum exhibits use design to combine materials and create a product for an intended audience. Recipe development also uses design to combine ingredients and create food products for groups of people.

In both these instances, exhibits and recipes meet the needs of others as well as those who design them. Exhibits meet the needs of visitors as well as the desires of the museum curators who work on their design. Recipes meet the needs of others and the person who selected and cooked the recipe.

Integrating multiple needs is what exhibit evaluative methods work to resolve and can be adapted for recipe selection and development as well. This chapter borrows from exhibit design and creative other fields to illustrate ways to produce food that people want to eat.

The process of recipe development is explored to identify questions that might be asked along the way to improve the overall cooking experience. Recipe outcomes are discussed beyond a food's taste to broaden the scope of evaluation efforts.

Integrating Multipe Needs

Museum exhibit designers use front-end evaluation to provide information early in the process to ensure that input from those affected is incorporated into the design (Donnelly, Chang-Yu, Biswas, Ying, Denny, and Hodge, 2010). Front-end evaluation explores what visitors want to learn from an exhibit and is carried out before any major content decisions are made.

Formative evaluation makes improvements during developmental phases (Wholey, Hatry, and Newcomer, 2004). Formative evaluation in exhibit design tests the effectiveness of an exhibit's message during the planning stage and usually involves interviews or focus groups to gather input. Formative evaluation, for example, asks visitors if a sign showing an image of a pond in the woods conveys the message that woodlands are more than just trees.

Summative evaluation gauges the exhibit's effectiveness after completion and usually involves the use of quantitative methods, such as written surveys. Applied to cooking, front-end evaluation gathers opinions on the type of food to be cooked. In a dinner situation, people can be asked their entrée preferences that determine the animal or vegetable protein used. Preferences on the cooking method can also be discussed.

Once questions like these are answered, formative evaluation assesses people's reaction to a recipe that combines the chosen protein type and cooking method. If the protein is fish and the method is a sauté, reaction is measured to a recipe for Sautéed East Coast Flounder with a Lemon Garlic Almond Sauce.

Once met with approval, the fish is cooked and summative evaluation gathers opinions on the flavor outcome that includes, aroma, taste, and texture. This information informs future recipe development that may include other fish dishes that are closely related. Gathering input at the beginning eliminates guesswork and prevents a dish being made that people actually do not want.

Gaining recipe approval confirms the cooking direction based on the ingredients and methods determined up front. Evaluation at the end looks at what worked and what did not based on people's reactions.

Gathering input along the way through front end, formative, and summative evaluation continually works to avoid problems that result from decisions made in a vacuum.

Evaluating the Process

Recipe directions are not always followed as written or as originally planned. What is actually done may be quite different, sometimes leading to better results and hopefully not worse. The cooking method may be corrected to reflect what is written instead of what is described. During preparation, methods and techniques may have been layered in to provide additional flavor.

These dynamic changes and the reasons behind them are what process evaluation considers. Evaluation focuses on the process to see if the approaches taken are operating as planned (Zint, 2013). Process evaluation takes place throughout recipe development and cooking or is completed as a one-time assessment after the outcome has been reached. Evaluation many times takes the form of mental or written notes that are fully considered after cooking has been completed.

One area to evaluate that takes place before cooking begins is recipe selection. People usually have a favorite source for recipe information. Exploring these places for ideas is part of the recipe selection process. If the Internet is the source for recipe ideas, did the findings produce the intended result? Was searching online a good use of time or would the effort be better spent reviewing books or magazines or talking with family members or friends?

If recipe conversion was used to assess ingredient relationships, did the process go as planned? Research is an important component of recipe conversion that finds answers to questions not addressed in the recipe directions. Were ingredient choices or adjustments made as a direct result of research input? What additional resources are needed in the future to make the process work more smoothly? Would input from other people have been helpful in resolving any issues? Were substitutions made for ingredients that were thought to be on hand? Could this situation be avoided in the future using a different approach?

Process evaluation also looks beyond procedural aspects and considers the setting in which decisions are made. Was working at a desk the best place to think through issues or is the kitchen a better environment?

Looking at the cooking process, specific aspects probably come to mind immediately. Before exploring these details, start broadly and assess how the overall process functioned. Simply stated, did cooking go as planned? Did recipe directions describe what really happened? Was the experience stressful? If yes, what are the reasons behind this anxiety? Can these factors be controlled or were they unexpected interruptions that could not directly be planned for in the future?

Did the level of organization play a role in having the cooking process unfold smoothly? Were ingredients scaled, assembled, and laid out before cooking began? If weighing ingredients for the first time, how did the experience compare with using cups and spoon measures? Is this manner of measuring ingredients something that could or should be incorporated into other recipes?

The tools used in food preparation and cooking affect the development of the final product. Was new equipment purchased or was the recipe made with tools already on hand? The best new gadget can make preparation easier or just become another tool lost in a drawer among many others.

The cooking process also includes recipe documentation for those who wish to formalize the process more thoroughly. If using a smartphone to photograph the process, what are the strengths and weaknesses of this piece of equipment? Did photographing procedures interrupt the process, breaking the rhythm experienced in moving through each step in the procedure?

Questions like these are just a few that help to evaluate the process to select, develop, and cook a recipe. The answers can be used to improve future experiences and help meet individual needs.

Evaluating Recipe Outcomes

Evaluating recipe flavor is routinely practiced after cooking or food preparation. Specific goals can be set for a food's texture or aroma and later evaluated after cooking. Fluffy mashed potatoes may be the goal that research provides various methods of preparation to test.

Recipes are developed, prepared, and cooked to see whether their outcomes meet expectations. Ingredient ratios may be changed to create flavor balance in a recipe that, once the food is eaten, may need further adjustment or may have met the goal.

Goal setting motivates some people to complete what they have started, but it also can lead to thoughts of failure when things do not work out as planned. A goal-free environment focuses on what happened instead of what was supposed to happen. If one method of preparation results in lumpy mashed potatoes, the result is not a failure but the lessons learned can inform future directions.

Recipe flavor outcomes are often described qualitatively, that is, they take the form of descriptions that come from observation. People often comment on what they are eating without even being asked their opinion. This type of response is probably the most often encountered when assessing recipe flavor.

The same dish served to multiple people may elicit a range of responses since evaluation is a subjective measure. These opinions may vary by a person's age, gender, or a prior flavor experience with the same or a similar dish. Those who are not aware of recipe details may limit their comments to their level of enjoyment during the eating experience.

Initial flavor outcomes change over time. The phrase, "It tastes better the next day," is used for foods whose flavor profile improves over time. Flavors can deepen as a result of concentration or reduction as liquids evaporate with cooling before refrigeration. Additionally, reheating helps to release the aromas in food.

Recipe flavor outcomes are also evaluated quantitatively. Quantitative data are measured numerically. These methods can actually be used to capture subjective opinions with numbers. Rating scales used by professional tasters (Stuckey, 2012) evaluate preferences for different foods. These data are actually quantitative because they are designed to capture changes in magnitude and not opinion. Scales are numbered in equal intervals representing an ordering such as dislike extremely to like extremely. In this instance, a nine-point scale separates these two extremes. Rating scale data lend themselves to analysis by statistical measures over paragraphs of written descriptions that are qualitative in nature.

Quantitative methods are probably more familiar in the context of recipe yields that are calculated to meet the food needs of a specific-sized group of people. A recipe that was supposed to feed five people but only feeds three produces a problematic outcome. The lack of portion size in many consumer recipes increases the chance for errors in the number of servings produced.

Recipes are also evaluated in terms of how much time, effort, or cost is required to produce an intended outcome. Sauces that are thickened through reduction take long periods of time to produce. Slurries and roux are thickening agents that achieve similar results but in less time.

These savings in time are not without consequences. These agents can alter the appearance, taste, and texture of sauces and are not equivalent to evaporation methods. The amount of time saved needs to be evaluated in the context of any flavor changes to the sauce under consideration.

With the abundance of cooking equipment available today, the choice of one type over another should be evaluated in the context of the output produced. Purchasing a three hundred dollar French-made Dutch oven does not save any cooking time over a less expensive version. Construction differences may be a reason for purchasing one over the other but not time-saving or producing a better-tasting product. Professional kitchens may use large capacity aluminum pots that are more versatile across dishes than spending resources on specialized higher-cost cast iron equipment.

Spending hours finding and purchasing an ingredient for a recipe that uses only a small portion of the product is probably not the most efficient use of time and resources. Recipe outcomes are usually framed in terms of recipe flavor, but outcomes can also be measured in terms of the time, effort, and cost that were incurred to produce an intended result.

What You've Been Missing in Recipe Evaluation

Evaluation looks at both the intended and unexpected occurrences that happen in the process of recipe development and cooking, and it gathers input from the people being served. Recipe evaluation is often limited to the assessment of food taste. Undertaken when cooking has finished, a simple thumb up or down on recipe outcomes signals a person is done and can move onto the next thing.

The information gained through more comprehensive evaluation efforts identifies areas for improvement, offers insight into the best use of time and resources, and ensures that cooking decisions are not made in a vacuum. Evaluation is something that should be embraced and made an integral part of recipe selection, development, and cooking. What is missing from recipe evaluation?

- Evaluation can lead to increased knowledge, skills, and changes in attitudes that open up new ways of thinking about recipes.

- Front-end recipe evaluation gathers input before any major decisions are made to ensure the food produced is what people want. Input early-on influences recipe selection and guards against decisions being made in a vacuum.

- Formative recipe evaluation provides confirmation on recipe direction or encourages the search for alternatives that more closely fit the need.

- Summative recipe evaluation gathers opinions on recipe outcomes that inform future cooking decisions.

- Process evaluation assesses what happened during recipe development, preparation, and cooking against what was planned. Insights gained can be applied to future endeavors to produce better outcomes.

- Recipe outcomes can be evaluated against predefined goals. Goal setting motivates people to complete what they start, but it also can lead to disappointment when results do not match expectations.

- Goal-free recipe evaluation learns from what happened. Recipe outcomes are viewed as valuable whether they come out as planned or are unexpected.

- Qualitative and quantitative methods are used to evaluate flavor outcomes of recipes.

- Evaluation of recipe outcomes includes an assessment of the time, effort, or cost that produces a given output. These measures look at the efficiency of the process and use quantitative measures to assess the data.

EVALUATION

RECIPES

Chapter Six

Summary
A Framework for Recipe Interpretation

In a perfect world, every recipe would come out as pictured or described, but reality supports the opposite as being true. People face unexpected outcomes and are left disappointed or feel they did something wrong. Is this situation "the way of the world" or can problematic recipes be revised before they are produced?

Correction is possible, but more often people just avoid "bad" recipes by following the recommendations of others. Recipes from the Internet are used only if they receive four or five star ratings. Recipe selection is limited to well known magazines, books, family, and friends, or those by television chefs of notoriety.

These strategies are good places to start, but they leave recipe ingredient, technique, and method choices to others. Some people want these decisions to be made for them, but that requires faith in the author's approach and hope that the outcome will be as expected.

Others select recipes by looking at their clarity, complexity, length of time to produce, visual appearance, and quantity of output. This approach personalizes the selection process, but it may also lead to unexpected results. In some cases, important recipe information is missing or, if available, is not in a form that is easily accessible.

Without a process to uncover what is missing, important information goes unnoticed and leads to unexpected outcomes. The design process unlocks the inner workings of recipes and reveals ingredient relationships, flavor development, techniques, and methods. The process is not linear but involves cycles of defining problems and developing their solutions. The process views recipes as problematic and in need of better answers.

Research sheds light on any unknown variables and clarifies the issues at hand. Concepts broadly filter recipe components and define an approach to resolve identified problems. Design makes hard decisions and determines a culinary direction. Testing works to validate design decisions and evaluation looks at the entire process and outcomes. Resulting recipe solutions are built on insight and learning that inform future recipe decisions.

Incorporated into a larger framework for recipe interpretation, the design process helps people avoid potential problems and produces better outcomes. The framework (Figure 6-1) consists of six stages of examination and recipe interpretation

Step 1 Determine Recipe Type

There are two basic types of recipes: those for professionals and those for consumers. Recipes that provide yield, portion size, and ingredient weight point in the direction of a professional recipe. The presence of cup and spoon measures or directions that take the form of stories suggest consumer recipes.

Identifying the recipe type prepares the user for what lies ahead in terms of information accuracy and completeness. Professional recipes are accurate but may not provide much recipe detail or may include culinary jargon. On the other hand, anything goes as far as content is concerned in consumer recipes.

Step 2 Examine the Recipe Structure

Conceptual development identifies ingredient functions, techniques, and cooking methods. Ingredients impart flavor or support development of flavor in recipes. Research on their pairings or groupings may suggest strong affiliations with each other.

On the other hand, analysis may uncover flavor imbalances or conflicts. The timing of ingredient additions may reveal layering strategies to develop flavor depth. Techniques, methods and ingredients develop flavor in recipes.

Methods should be supported by recipe techniques if they are part of the recipe title. Sequencing of methods and techniques may reveal layering strategies that develop flavor depth. Input from others in this early stage of recipe selection may provide confirmation on the recipe direction. Broad review of recipe ingredients, techniques, and methods should provide enough information to weed out many recipes and identify problem areas that may require further attention.

Step 3 Assess Ingredient Relationships

Design examines ingredient relationships to see if they fall within accepted culinary norms or support personal flavor preferences. Consumer recipes require conversion from cup and spoon measures to ounces and pounds. Once this work is completed, ingredient ratios and percentages are analyzed.

In some cases, known standards are available to compare against. Otherwise, analysis looks for common patterns or differences in ingredient use between recipes. Nutritional analysis using computer software also helps to differentiate recipes that appear to be similar. Based on these findings and the ideas associated with them, a decision is made to move ahead or make changes to the recipes under consideration.

Step 4 Test Recipe Decisions

Testing takes the form of cooking or recipe assembly based on the decisions made to that point. The act of cooking is the focus of much of what people see and read about in books, magazines, and television shows.

Step 5 Evaluate

Evaluation looks at both recipe outcomes and the development process to see if changes could be made to make things better the next time. Evaluation can be a one-time event after cooking but is more useful when carried out throughout the recipe selection, development, and cooking stages.

Step 6 Document Results

Recipe information is documented or revised. The lessons learned should be written down since they can be used to inform future cooking endeavors. Information can be laid out in documents that use text only or include photographs. The process begins again when a new recipe is considered for

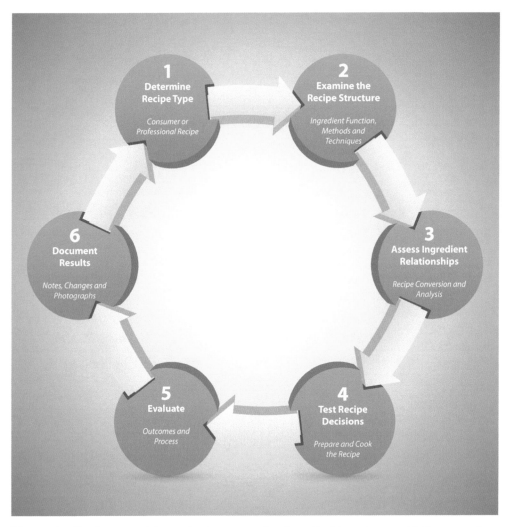

Figure 6-1 The framework for recipe interpretation is cyclical in nature and follows a series of steps to develop a recipe that meets the needs under consideration.

development.

Although recipe directions describe a linear process from beginning to completion, the development of a great recipe is not as straight forward. Each step along the way is subject to change as a result of recipe interpretation. Some of your findings will steer you away from poorly developed recipes saving both time and effort. Other times recipe changes result in better outcomes. To meet your needs recipes may have to be tested at least twice.

Take a curious approach and use a rational mind to guide your way through new cooking situations. Recipe interpretation encourages problem solving and helps you to accept answers that are different from what was originally expected. Such results, though challenging, often lead to tremendous and meaningful discoveries. There are many things missing from recipes but now you know the nature of these problems as well as ways and sources of information to help correct recipe issues. Good cooking!

RECIPES

Appendix I
Weights of Common Produce

Vegetables, fruits, and herbs are difficult to measure because of their natural variability. Terms such as medium-sized are used to quantify these ingredients, but in the end are subjective measures. Dimensions more accurately describe vegetable size but are typically not provided in recipes.

The table in this appendix contains the untrimmed sizes and weights of many vegetables, fruits, and herbs that have been sourced at a retail grocery store. Qualitative descriptions, such as small, medium and large, are used but are accompanied by specific ingredient dimensions.

Data were collected with an adjustable hand-held caliper, a ruler, and a digital scale with an accuracy of .05 ounces. Strong tapering or irregular-shaped root vegetables, such as ginger, are not included. Dimensions describe the majority of the vegetable and do not extend to the root ends or leaves.

Herbs are difficult to measure because of their irregular branching pattern and leaf arrangement. The term sprig is often used in recipes to quantify fresh herbs and describes a small branch or shoot. There is not an accepted standard for a sprig, making the choice of branch selection a matter of personal preference or using cut-to-size, pre-packaged herbs in stores. Four commonly used herbs were measured using this latter form as a standard.

Figure A-1 Single & branched forms of thyme sprigs.

Common Thyme (*Thymus vulgaris*) can be used as a single or multiple-branched form of the same length (Figure A-1). Oreganos form a group of about twenty perennials that are native to the Mediterranean and East Asia (Rodd & Bryant, 2007). Wild oregano (*Origanum vulgare*), also known as wild marjoram, has several species that range in their aromatic qualities. Italian oregano (*Origanum majoricum*) has a thyme-like flavor. Bown (2001) describes Greek oregano (*Origanum onites*) as having inferior flavor. More common is the form of Greek oregano (*Origanum vulgare subsp. hirtum*) that is imported from Turkey and is grown as an herb in home gardens (MBOT, 2013). This subspecies can be used as an individual or multi-branched stem (Figure A-2).

Flat-leaf parsley (*Petroselinum crispum neapolitanum*) and curly-leaf parsley (*Petroselinum crispum*) are regularly used in culinary dishes. Flat-leaf parsley has larger leaves (Figure A-3) that can easily be removed to create a parsley stem used in stock development. Although both could be used to flavor recipes, curly-leaf parsley is used more as a garnish than a flavoring (Tucker & DeBaggio, 2009). An exception is its use in Tabbouleh, a Lebanese salad that is often made with curly-leaf parsley. Rosemary (*Rosarinus officinalis*) is used as a

Figure A-2 Single stemmed oregano sprig

Figure A-3 Italian flat-leaved parsley sprig

Figure A-4 Single-stemmed rosemary sprig.

single-stem herb that can be cut to a variety of lengths (Figure A-4).

The As-Purchased (AP) weight of a product refers to its delivered form in a food service operation (Dopson, Hayes & Miller, 2008). For home use, the AP weight is the purchased amount at a local grocery store. The portion that is actually used in both professional and home kitchens is called the edible portion. This amount is less than the As-Purchased weight unless every bit of an item is used. Stocks, for example, can be made with onions that include their skins and root-ends – letting nothing go to waste. In this case, the As-Purchased weight should be given in the recipe and a note made to indicate all parts of the onion are used.

More commonly, recipes require only a portion of an item be used. In the case of leeks, typically only the white end is consumed and the green tops are discarded or used in stock development. In this case, the weight of the white end (edible portion) should be provided and not the AP weight that includes the green leaves.

The weights and dimensions of many common vegetables, fruits, and herbs are listed in the table that follows (Table 1.0). The weights of most items are rounded to the nearest ounce. Smaller items are scaled to the nearest half-ounce. Small items and herbs are scaled to two decimal points. Table information is meant to serve as a guide and not a definitive source of size or weight information. Vegetables not only vary naturally by size, but weight variances result from differences in product freshness and how the item was stored.

Table 1.0
Weights of Common Vegetables, Fruits, and Herbs

Produce	Dimensions	Ounces
A		
Apple - Fuji	3.25" dia. x 2.75" high	8.5 oz.
Apple - Granny Smith	3.5" dia. x 3" high	9 oz.
Apple - Granny Smith (small)	2.75" dia. x 2.5" high	5.5 oz.
Apple - Honey Crisp	3.75" dia. x 3" high	11 oz.
Apple - Honey Crisp (small)	2.75" dia. x 2.5" high	5.5 oz.
Apricot - fresh	2.25" dia. x 2.5" high	4.5 oz.
Artichoke	4.5" dia. x 5" high (2.5" stem)	13.5 oz.
Avocado	3" dia. x 4" long	9 oz.
B		
Banana	1.5" wide x 10" long	8 oz.
Beet - no leaves	3" dia. x 2.75" high	8 oz.
Beet - no leaves (large)	4" dia. x 3.25" high	16 oz.
Bok Choy - baby	3" wide x 9" long	9 oz.
Brussels Sprout (small)	1" dia. x 1.5" high	.45 oz.
Brussels Sprout (medium)	2" dia. x 2" high	1.5 oz.
Brussels Sprout (large)	2.25" dia. x 4" long	3 oz.
C		
Cabbage (head)	6" dia. x 5" high	36 oz.
Cabbage - napa (medium)	4.5" dia. x 7" long	40 oz.
Cantaloupe	5.75" dia. x 5.75" high	54 oz.
Cauliflower (small)	4" dia. x 5" high	28 oz.
Cauliflower (medium)	6.5" dia. x 4" high	45 oz.

Produce	Dimensions	Ounces
Carrot - bagged (small)	1.25" dia. x 5.5" long	2.5 oz.
Carrot - bagged (medium)	1.25" dia. x 8" long	3.5 oz.
Carrot - bulk (large)	2" dia. x 10.5" long	10 oz.
Celeriac Root (small)	3.5" dia. x 3.5" high	10.5 oz.
Celeriac Root (large)	5.75" dia. x 4.5" high	35 oz.
Celery Stalk - no leaves	2.5" base x 1" wide x 13" long	3.5 oz.
Coconut	5" dia. x 6" high	30 oz.
Corn - with husk (small)	1.75" dia. x 7" long	8.5 oz.
Corn - with husk	2.25" dia. x 9" long	13 oz.
Corn - Chinese baby	5/8" dia. x 3.5" long	.40 oz.
Cucumber (medium)	2" dia. x 8" long	10.5 oz.
Cucumber (large)	2" dia. x 10.5" long	17.5 oz.
Cucumber - English	1.75" dia. x 11.5" long	11.5 oz.
D		
Daikon (small)	2.25" dia. x 9" long	15 oz.
Daikon (medium)	2" dia. x 17" short taper	20 oz.
E		
Eggplant (small)	3" dia. x 6" long	10 oz.
Eggplant (medium)	3.5" dia. x 8.5" long	19 oz.
Eggplant (large)	4.25" dia. x 9" long	30 oz.
Eggplant - Chinese	1.75" dia. x 9.5" long	7 oz.
Eggplant - Ichiban	1.5" dia. x 6" long	3.5 oz.
Escarole - head	6" dia. x 6" high	17 oz.
F		
Fava Bean Pod	1.25" wide x 6.5" long	1.5 oz.
Fennel Bulb - stalks & leaves	3.5" dia. x 3.5" high x 18" tall	22 oz.
Frisée	3.5" dia. x 4" high	4 oz.
G		
Garlic - head (small)	2" dia. x 1.5" tall	1.5 oz.
Garlic - head	2.75 " dia. x 2" tall	3 oz.
Gobo Root - Taiwan	1.25" dia. x 35" long	28.5 oz.
Gobo Root - Japan	.75" dia. x 26" long	10 oz.

Produce	Dimensions	Ounces
Grapefruit	4" dia. x 3.5" high	13 oz.
H		
Honeydew Melon	4" dia. x 3.5" high	60 oz.
J		
Jicama	4.5" dia. x 3" high	18 oz.
K		
Kabocha	5.75" dia. x 3.25" high	26 oz.
Kiwi Fruit	2.5" dia. x 3" long	4 oz.
L		
Leek - no leaves	1.5" dia. x 15" long	13 oz.
Lemon (medium)	2.5" dia. x 3" long	5 oz.
Lemon (large)	3" dia. x 4" long	8.5 oz.
Lemongrass - stem	3/4" dia. x 18" long	2 oz.
Lettuce - iceberg head	6" dia. round	22 oz.
Lime	2.25" dia. x 2.5" high	4 oz.
Lotus Root - Renkon	2.25" dia. x 4.25" long	5 oz.
M		
Mango	3.5" dia. x 4.5" long	16 oz.
Mushroom - button (small)	1.5" dia. x 1.5" high	.5 oz.
Mushroom - button	2.25" dia. x 1.75" high	1 oz.
N		
Negi (Japanese green onion)	.75" dia. x 29" long	6 oz.
O		
Onion - Spanish (small)	3" dia. x 3" high	9 oz.
Onion - Spanish (medium)	3.5" dia. x 3" high	11.5 oz.
Onion - Spanish (large)	3.75" dia. x 3.75" high	17 oz.
Onion - white (medium)	3.5" dia. x 3" high	10 oz.
Onion - white (large)	3.75" dia. x 3.75" high	13 oz.
Orange - navel	3.25" dia. x 3.5" high	10 oz.
Oregano (sprig)	1" wide x 5" long	.10 oz.
P		
Parsley flat-leaved (sprig)	3" wide x 7" long	.15 oz.

Produce	Dimensions	Ounces
Parsley Stem	1/8" dia. x 3.75" long	.04 oz.
Parsnip	1.5" dia. x 8.5" long	6 oz.
Parsnip (large)	2.75" dia. - 1.75" dia. x 8" long	13 oz.
Pear - Bartlett	3" dia. x 4" high	8 oz.
Pear - Hosui	3.75" dia. x 3.25" high	16 oz.
Pepper - Banana	1.75" dia. x 5.5 " long	2.5 oz.
Pepper - Bell (small)	3" dia. x 3" high	7 oz.
Pepper - Bell	4" dia. x 5" high	13 oz.
Pepper - Jalapeno (small)	1" dia. x 2.5" long	1 oz.
Pepper - Jalapeno (medium)	1.5" dia. x 3" long	1.5 oz.
Pepper - Jalapeno (large)	1.5" dia. x 4" long	2 oz.
Pepper - Habanero	1.75" dia. x 2" long	.50 oz.
Pepper - Red Ancient Sweet	2" wide x 8" long	2.5 oz.
Persimmon	3" dia. x 2.25" high	7.5 oz.
Persimmon - Kaki	3" dia. x 1.75" high	5.75 oz.
Pineapple (including crown)	5" dia. x 6.5" high (fruit only)	63 oz.
Pomegranate	4" dia. x 3.5" high	18 oz.
Potato - Red	3" dia. x 3" long	5.5 oz.
Potato - Russet (medium)	3" dia. x 5" long	10 oz.
Potato - Satoimo	2.75" dia. x 5" long	10 oz.
R		
Rhubarb stem (no leaves)	1.25" wide x 16" long	5 oz.
Rosemary Sprig	1" wide x 6.5" long	.15 oz.
Rosemary Sprig (small)	1" wide x 4" long	.05 oz.
Rutabaga (medium)	4.25" dia. x 3.75" high	18 oz.
Rutabaga (large)	5" dia. x 5.5 " high	38 oz.
S		
Shallot - whole	2.25" wide x 3" long	3.5 oz.
Squash - Acorn	5" dia. x 6" long	28 oz.
Squash - Butternut (medium	4" dia. base - 3.25" dia. top x 8"	30 oz.
Squash - Butternut (large)	5.75" dia. base - 4" dia. top x 11"	76 oz.
Squash - Summer	2" dia. x 7" length	7.5 oz.

Produce	Dimensions	Ounces
Star Fruit - Carambola	3" dia. x 4.5" long	6.5 oz.
T		
Tangerine	3" dia. x 2.5" high	7 oz.
Taro Root - Eddoe	3" dia. x 3.5" high	11 oz.
Thyme Sprig	1" wide x 6" long - branched	.05 oz.
Tomatillo - with husk	2" dia. x 2" high	2 oz.
Tomatillo - with husk (large)	2.75" dia. x 2.5" high	5 oz.
Tomato (small)	2.5" dia. x 2.25" high	4.5 oz.
Tomato	3.25" dia. x 2.75" high	9 oz.
Tomato - Roma (small)	2" dia. x 2.5" high	3.5 oz.
Tomato - Roma	2.5" dia. x 3" high	6.5 oz.
Turnip (small)	2.5" dia. x 2" high	4 oz.
Turnip (medium)	3.5" dia. x 3" high	12 oz.
Turnip (large)	4.25 " dia. x 3.5" high	15 oz.
Y		
Yam	2.5" dia. x 7.5" long	14 oz.
Yucca Root	3.5" dia. - 2.5" dia. x 12" long	45 oz.
Z		
Zucchini (medium)	1.75" dia. x 8.5" long	9.5 oz.
Zucchini (large)	2.25" dia. x 9" long	13.5 oz.

RECIPES

Appendix II
Table of Flavor Relationships

Flavor is made up of taste, aroma, and texture. Of these three components, taste is something that you are probably familiar with and comfortable talking about with others. Its effect on flavor development is more easily recognized than the influence of technique and cooking method.

Knowing which tastes work well together helps to recognize recipes with balanced flavors. Identifying these favorable pairings early in recipe selection assures that the outcome is what is desired. A cheeseburger is a good example that pairs umami with umami in the partnering of browned beef and melted cheese ingredients.

On the other hand, bitterness is a taste that should be balanced. Recipes that contain bitter-tasting ingredients are commonly offset by sweetness or saltiness. Bitter salad greens like watercress can be balanced by the sweetness of apples. Salt sprinkled on fresh radishes subdues their inherent bitterness. Finding omissions or unfavorable pairings in an ingredient list may suggest that recipe changes should be considered.

The Table of Flavor Relationships (Table 1.0) summarizes favorable pairings for the five tastes and examples are provided as well. Suggestions are also made to enhance the aroma and texture of foods.

Table 1.0
Table of Flavor Relationships

Flavor	Relationship	Taste	Ingredient Type	Example	Comment
Saltiness	Subdues	Bitterness		Radishes	Salted Radishes
	Pairs with	Sweetness		Caramel	Salted Caramel Apples
	Pairs with	Umami		Cured Meats	Chicken Soup with Bacon
	Balanced by	Sourness	Acid	Lemon & Vinegar	Salt and Malt Vinegar Roasted Potatoes
	Too Salty fix with		Fats and Starches	Cream, Milk, Yogurt, Potatoes	Dilutes Salt Concentration or Absorbs Dissolved Salts
	Excessively Salty fix by				Doubling Recipe Quantity
Bitterness	Pairs with		Fats	Meats	Collard Greens and Smoked Ham Hocks
	Pairs with	Sourness		Tomato	Tomatoes and Garlic Pasta
	Balanced by	Sweetness		Fruits	Watercress and Gala Apple Salad
	Balanced by	Saltiness		Salt	Salted Grapefruit
Sourness	Pairs with		Fats	Oils	Vinaigrette Salad Dressing
	Pairs with	Saltiness		Salt	Preserved Grape Leaves
	Pairs with	Sweetness	Fructose	Fruits	Balsamic Vinegar Sprinkled on Fresh Strawberries
	Brightens		Starches	Rice	Gremolata and Risotto
	Brightens		Fats	Meats	Vinegar with Meat Sauces
Sweetness	Pairs with	Sourness		Vinegar	Sweet and Sour Chicken
	Pairs with		Fats	Butter	Lobster and Butter

Flavor	Relationship	Taste	Ingredient Type	Example	Comment
Sweetness	Pairs with	Bitterness		Sage	Blackberry and Sage Amaranth Pancakes
	Too Sweet fix with	Sourness Sweetness Saltiness		Lemon Fruit Juice Honey Salt	Add Lemon Juice to Meat Sauces. Substitute Honey for Refined Sugars.
Umami	Pairs with	Umami		Tomato	Baked Parmesan Tomatoes
Piquancy	Too hot fix with		Fats	Cream	Fattiness Binds Oils
	Balanced by	Sweetness		Honey	Honey Mustard Sauce
Texture	Watery fix with			Reduction	Sauce Evaporation
	Too Watery fix with		Thickeners	Cornstarch and Water or Flour and Butter	Slurry and Roux
Aroma	Too low fix with			Bread	Heat in Oven Briefly

RECIPES

Appendix III
Table of Ingredients by Taste Profile

Developing flavor involves more than just knowing which of the five tastes work well together. Just because sweetness pairs with bitterness does not mean that Chinese hoisin sauce mixed with coffee go together well.

Decisions need to be made within the context of the recipe. An ingredient's form and its role in flavor development also need to be considered. Spices often come dried, finely ground, and work in conjunction with other ingredients to develop flavor. People do not eat a teaspoon of ground cumin for its flavor experience.

Taste profiles for many ingredients can be found in books and on the Internet but are not often organized by their type. Spices, vegetables, and fruits represent different food categories but are often listed together. Allspice and carrots may be included on the same list because of their sweet taste but most pairing decisions are not based on taste alone.

The ingredient tables in this appendix are not only differentiated by taste, but also by type to assist in making pairing decisions.

The table on salty-tasting ingredients (Table 1.0) focuses on raw and not processed foods. Cooked, canned, or otherwise pre-processed ingredients often have salt added that greatly increases their natural sodium content.

Anchovies are known for their saltiness in their canned form. These fish contain significantly less sodium in their natural form. The amount of sodium in Chili powder may surprise those who use the spice for its flavor and not its sodium content.

Bitter-tasting ingredients (Table 2.0) are missing examples in some categories. There are no bitter grains or sweeteners listed. Unpopulated fields are also found in most of the other charts.

The table on sour-tasting foods (Table 3.0) may have ingredients that are not familiar. Cornelian cherries are berries that are not widely used in recipes, but is a common landscape plant used in hedges and other situations where screening of unwanted views is needed.

The table on sweet-tasting ingredients (Table 4.0) list some fruits that may be both sour and sweet-tasting at the same time. Purchased in grocery stores, many of the fruits are probably sour-tasting because they are picked before they are fully ripened.

The fifth table on umami (Table 5.0) contains a smaller assortment of ingredients than the other tables. This shows the limited nature of where umami occurs naturally in foods.

Please note that many of the ingredients are found on more than one table. Bacon is an ingredient that is salty and also has an umami taste.

Botanically speaking, plant fruits are developed from their flowers. Some vegetables are actually fruits, like tomatoes, but they are listed as a vegetable since people do not often find tomatoes mixed in with the apples and oranges in local supermarkets.

APPENDIX III

Table 1.0
Table of Salty-Tasting Ingredients

Fruits	Vegetables	Herbs	Grains	Spices
Lemons, Preserved 1333mg/100g	Capers, Canned 2,769mg/100g	Parsley, Dried 452mg/100g	Cornmeal, Self-Rising, En-riched, Yellow 1,348mg/100g	Chili Powder 4,000mg/100g
Olives, Ripe, Canned 735mg/100g	Pickles, Cucumber 875mg/100g	Spearmint, Dried 344 mg/100g		Cloves, Ground 277mg/100g
	Wakame Raw 872mg/100g	Coriander Leaf, Dried 211 mg/100g		Cumin Seed, Dried 168mg/100g
	Tomatoes, Sun-Dried 247mg/100g	Dill Weed, Dried 208mg/100g		Celery Seed 160mg/100g
	Beet Greens, Raw 233mg/100g	Chervil, Dried 83mg/100g		Saffron 148mg/100g
	Seaweed, Kelp Raw 233mg/100g	Marjoram, Dried 77mg/100g		Fennel Seed 88mg/100g
	Swiss Chard, Raw 213 mg/100g	Basil, Dried 76mg/100g		Mace, Ground 80mg/100g
	Artichokes, Raw 94mg/100g			
	New Zealand Spinach, Raw 130mg/100g			
	Celeriac Root Raw 100mg/100g			
	Artichokes, Raw 94mg/100g			
	Peppers, hot Chili, Sun-Dried 91mg/100g			
	Celery Raw 90mg/100g			
	Spinach, Raw 79mg/100g			

Fats & Dairy	Sweeteners	Flavorings	Nuts	Proteins
Pecorino Cheese 1,940 mg/100g		Salt, Table 38,758 mg/100g		Mackerel, Salted 4,450 mg/100g
Roquefort Cheese 1,809 mg/100g		Fish Sauce 7,851mg/100g		Prosciutto 2,199 mg/100g
Parmesan Shredded 1,696 mg/100g		Soy Sauce, Soy & Wheat Based 5,493mg/100g		Pancetta 1,607 mg/100g
Romano Cheese 1,433mg/100g		Miso 3,728 mg/100g		Ham, Cured, Whole, Lean, Unheated 1,516 mg/100g
Parmesan Cheese, Hard 1,376mg/100g		Oyster Sauce 2,733mg/100g		Chorizo 1,235 mg/100g
Swiss Cheese, Pasteurized 1,370mg/100g		Hoisin Sauce 1,615mg/100g		Salami, Cooked Beef 1,140 mg/100g
Blue Cheese 1,146mg/100g				Anchovies, Can 1,040mg/100g
Gorgonzola Cheese 1,088 mg/100g				Crab, Alaska King Raw 836 mg/100g
Cheddar Cheese 1,000 mg/100g				Bacon, Cured, Uncooked 662 mg/100g
Feta Cheese 917mg/100g				Clams, Raw 601 mg/100g
Provolone Cheese 876 mg/100g				
Camembert Cheese 842 mg/100g				
Gouda Cheese 819mg/100g				

Table 2.0
Table of Bitter-Tasting Ingredients

Fruits	Vegetables	Herbs	Grains	Spices
Cranberries	Artichokes	Angelica		Caraway Seed
Grapefruit	Arugula	Chicory		Celery Seed
Lemon Zest	Bok Choy	Epazote		Cumin
Olives	Broccoli	Fenugreek		Curry Powder
Orange Zest	Broccoli Rabe	Fiddlehead		Juniper Berries
	Brussels Sprouts	Garlic		Mustard Seed
	Cauliflower	Hyssop		Pepper, Black
	Chicory	Oregano		Saffron
	Cilantro	Rosemary		Sesame Seed
	Collard Greens	Sage		Turmeric
	Cucumbers, Raw	Tarragon		
	Dandelion	Thyme		
	Eggplant			
	Endive			
	Escarole			
	Fava Beans			
	Frisée			
	Ginger			
	Green Peppers			
	Kale			
	Lettuce, Romaine			
	Lima Beans			
	Mustard Greens			
	Onions, Raw			
	Radicchio			
	Radish			
	Rhubarb			
	Spinach			
	Swiss Chard			
	Turnip Leaves			
	Turnips			
	Watercress			
	Zucchini			

Fats & Dairy	Sweeteners	Flavorings	Nuts	Proteins
		Beer	Almonds	Liver
		Chocolate	Pecans	
		Coffee	Walnuts	
		Mustard		
		Tea		
		Tonic Water		
		Wine		

Table 3.0
Table of Sour-Tasting Ingredients

Fruits	Vegetables	Herbs	Grains	Spices
Blackberries	Asparagus	Cilantro		Caraway Seeds
Blueberries	Cornichons	Dill		Coriander
Boysenberries	Cucumber Pickles	Galangal		Cream of Tartar
Caper Berries	Grape Leaves	Ginger		Curry Leaves
Cherries	Leeks	Lemon Balm		Ginger
Cornelian Cherries	Mushrooms, Enoki	Lemon Thyme		Saffron
Cranberries	Rhubarb	Lemongrass		Sumac
Currants	Tomatoes	Purslane		Tarragon
Granny Smith Apple	Tomatillos	Sorrel		
Grapefruit				
Grapes, Green				
Kaffir Lime				
Kiwi Fruit				
Kumquats				
Lemon				
Lemon, Preserved				
Lime				
Pomegranate				
Quince				
Tamarind				
Yuzu				

Fats & Dairy	Sweeteners	Flavorings	Nuts	Proteins
Buttermilk		Miso		Whey
Crème Fraiche		Ponzu		
Milk, Goat		Soy Sauce		
Sour Cream		Vinegar		
Yogurt		Wine		

Table 4.0
Table of Sweet-Tasting Ingredients

Fruits	Vegetables	Herbs	Grains	Spices
Apricots	Acorn Squash	Basil	Barley	Allspice
Bananas	Artichokes	Basil, Thai	Oatmeal	Cardamom
Blueberries	Beets	Bayleaf	Rice	Cinnamon
Clementines	Bell Peppers	Camomile	Wheat	Cloves
Currants	Butternut Squash	Caraway Seeds		Coriander
Dates	Carrots	Fennel		Five-Spice Powder
Figs	Corn	Lavender		Mace
Guava	Fennel	Mint		Marjoram
Juneberries	Garlic, Roasted			Nutmeg
Kiwi	Green Beans			Onion Powder
Mangoes	Jicama			Paprika
Melons	Kabocha			Parsley, Dried
Nectarines	Leeks			Poppy Seeds
Onions	Lotus Root			Sesame Seeds
Oranges	Onions, Vidalia			
Papaya	Parsnips			
Parsnips	Peas			
Passion Fruit	Pimentos			
Peaches	Potatoes			
Pears	Pumpkin			
Persimmons	Rutabagas			
Pimentos	Shallots			
Pineapple	Snap Peas			
Plantains	Sweet Potatoes			
Plums	Water Chestnut			
Prunes	Yam			
Raisins	Zucchini			
Strawberries				
Tangerines				
Watermelon				

Fats & Dairy	Sweeteners	Flavorings	Nuts	Proteins
Butter	Apple Cider	Hoisin Sauce	Almonds	Bass
Coconut Milk	Aspartame	Ketchup	Chestnuts	Beef
Cream	Brown Sugar	Licorice	Hazelnuts	Crab
Milk	Caramel	Madeira	Pine Nuts	Lamb
	Coconut	Malt		Lobster
	Corn Syrup	Maple Syrup		Mahi Mahi
	Hoisin Sauce	Mirin		Mussels
	Honey	Sake		Pork
	Maple Sugar	Sherry		Rabbit
	Maple Syrup	Vanilla		Scallops
	Molasses	Vermouth, Sweet		Shrimp
	Saccharine			
	Stevia			
	Sucralose			
	Sugar			

Table 5.0
Table of Umami-Tasting Ingredients

Fruits	Vegetables	Herbs	Grains	Spices
Grapefruit	Asparagus			
Grapes	Broccoli			
	Mushroom, Button			
	Carrots			
	Chinese Cabbage			
	Corn			
	Enokitake Mushrooms			
	Green Peas			
	Kelp (Kombu)			
	Mushrooms, Dried			
	Onion			
	Potatoes			
	Shitake Mushroom			
	Soy Beans			
	Sweet Potatoes			
	Tomatoes, Dried			
	Tomatoes			
	Truffles			
	Wakame			

Fats & Dairy	Sweeteners	Flavorings	Nuts	Proteins
Cheddar Cheese		Fish Sauce	Walnuts	Anchovies
Parmesan Cheese		Green Tea		Bacon
		Katsuobushi		Beef, Aged or Grilled
		Ketchup		Blue Crab
		Miso		Chicken
		Monosodium Glutamate		Cod
		Soy Sauce		Ham, Cured
		Stocks, Meat-Based		Lobster
		Vinegar, Balsamic		Mackerel
		Worcestershire Sauce		Oysters
				Pork
				Prawns
				Sardines
				Scallop
				Squid
				Tuna

RECIPES

References

About FoodNetwork.com: Food Network. (n.d.). *About FoodNetwork.com: Food network*. Retrieved February 12, 2014, from http://www.foodnetwork. com/site/about-foodnetwork-com.html.

Amendola, J., & Rees, N. (2003). Sugars and Other Sweeteners. *Understanding baking the art and science of baking* (3rd ed., p. 63). Hoboken, N.J.: J. Wiley.

Anderson, J. (2010). *Falling off the bone*. Hoboken, N.J.: John Wiley.

Barbour, M. G., Burk, J. H., & Pitts, W. D. (1987). Community Concepts and Attributes. *Terrestrial plant ecology* (2nd ed., p. 156). Menlo Park, Calif.: Benjamin/Cummings Pub. Co..

Bown, D. (2001). Origanum Species. *Herbal: the essential guide to herbs for living* (p. 189). New York: Barnes & Noble.

Brower, K. (2011). *Ingredient Pairings a Cooking Reference of Complimentary Ingredients*. U.S.A.: CreateSpace Independent Publishing Platform. Culinary Institute of America. (2008). *Garde Manger The Art and Craft of the Cold Kitchen*, (3rd ed.). Hoboken, N.J.: John Wiley.

Dirr, M. (1990). *Manual of woody landscape plants: their identification, ornamental characteristics, culture, propagation and uses* (4th ed.). Champaign, Ill.: Stipes Pub..

Dolson, L. (n.d.). Balancing and Blending Flavors in Food. *About.com low carb diets.* Retrieved May 2, 2014, from http://lowcarbdiets.about.com/od/cooking/a/flavorblending_3.htm.

Donnelly, A., Chang-Yu, W., Biswas, P., Ying, L., Denny, A., & Hodge, E. (2010). Front-End Evaluation to Enhance the Usefulness and Adoption of Educational Materials: from Museum Education to Engineering Education. *International Journal of Engineering Education*, 26(1), 155-161.

Dopson, L. R., Hayes, D. K., & Miller, J. E. (2008). Determining Actual and Attainable Product Costs. *Food and beverage cost control* (4th ed., p. 209). Hoboken, N.J.: John Wiley & Sons.

Dornenburg, A., & Page, K. (1996). *Culinary artistry.* New York: John Wiley.

Dornenburg, A., & Page, K. (2006). What to Eat with What you Drink. *What to drink with what you eat: the definitive guide to pairing food with wine, beer, spirits, coffee, tea-- even water-- based on expert advice from Americas best Sommeliers* (p. 80). New York: Bulfinch Press.

Eckbo, G. (1969). The Process of Landscape Development. *The landscape we see* (pp.11-13). New York: McGraw-Hill.

Food Group. (n.d.). *Agricultural Research Service United States Department of Agriculture.* Retrieved December 3, 2013, from http://ndb.nal.usda.gov/ndb/search/list.

Frechtling, J. A. (2007). Evaluation and Logic Models. *Logic modeling methods in program evaluation* (pp. 2-5). San Francisco: Jossey-Bass.
Goldstein, J. E. (1996). Introduction. *Kitchen conversations: robust recipes and lessons in flavor from one of America's most innovative chefs* (p. xxi). New York: Wm. Morrow.

Hamelman, J. (2004). Appendix. *Bread: a baker's book of techniques and recipes* (p. 376). Hoboken, N.J.: John Wiley.

Hemphill, I. (2002). Spice Notes. *The spice and herb bible: a cook's guide* (p. 127). Toronto: R. Rose.

Kikkoman Corporation. (n.d.). *Sensory check.* Retrieved April 21, 2014, from http://www.kikkoman.com/soysaucemuseum/difference/01.shtml.

Labensky, S. R., & Hause, A. M. (2007). *On cooking: a textbook of culinary fundamentals.* (4th ed.). Upper Saddle River, N.J.: Pearson Prentice Hall.

Lynch, Francis Talyn. *The book of yields: accuracy in food costing and purchasing.* 7th ed. Hoboken, N.J.: Wiley, 2008.

Menu Treats - Dairy Queen. (n.d.). *Dairy Queen.* Retrieved April 16, 2014, from http://www.dairyqueen.com/us-en/Menu/Treats/?localechange=1&&gcli d=CIyIm5LQ5b0CFexc.

MacGourmet Deluxe. (n.d.). *Mariner Software.* Retrieved December 3, 2013, from https://www.marinersoftware.com/products/macgourmet.

MacVeigh, J. (2009). Cuisines of Asia. *International cuisine* (p. 455). Clifton Park, NY: Delmar Cengage Learning.

McGee, H. (2004). Cooking Methods and Utensil Materials. *On food and cooking: the science and lore of the kitchen* (Completely rev. and updated ed., p. 778). New York: Scribner.

NDL/FNIC Food Composition Database Home Page. (n.d.). *Nutrient data laboratory/food and nutrition information center.* Retrieved December 2, 2013, from http://ndb.nal.usda.gov.

Nelson, J. K., & Zeratsky, K. (n.d.). Nutrition and healthy eating. *Fruit or vegetable — Do you know the difference?* Retrieved May 3, 2014, from http://www.mayoclinic.org/healthy-living/nutrition-and-healthy-eating/expert-blog/fruit-vegetable-difference/bgp-20056141.

Neves, C. M. (2002). *The making of exhibitions: purpose, structure, roles and process*. Washington, DC: Smithsonian Institution.

Olver, L. (n.d.). Food Timeline FAQs. *The food Timeline: history notes-- ice cream*. Retrieved April 17, 2014, from http://www.foodtimeline.org/ foodicecream.html.

Nisei Woman's Society, C. S. (1967). Salads and Tsukemono. *A taste of the orient* (p. 29). Fruitland, Idaho: Strange Printing Service.

Origanum vulgare subsp. hirtum - Plant Finder. (n.d.). *Origanum vulgare subsp. hirtum - plant finder*. Retrieved December 4, 2013, from http:// www.missouribotanicalgarden.org/PlantFinder/PlantFinderDetails. aspx?kempercode=q980.

Page, Karen, and Andrew Dornenburg. Flavor Matchmaking: The Charts. *The flavor bible: the essential guide to culinary creativity, based on the wisdom of America's most imaginative chefs*. New York: Little, Brown and Co., 2008. 91. Print.

Peterson, J. (2008). Liaisons and Overview. *Sauces: classical and contemporary sauce making* (3rd ed., p. 112). Hoboken, N.J.: Wiley.

Peterson, R. T. (1968). *Peterson first guide to wildflowers of northeastern and north-central North America* (p. 29). Boston: Houghton Mifflin

The professional chef (9th ed., p. 243). (2011). Stocks, Sauces, and Soups. Hoboken, N.J.: John Wiley & Sons.

Radhakrishna, R. B., & Relado, R. Z. (2009). A Framework to Link Evaluation Questions to Program Outcomes. *Journal of extension*, 47, 1-7. Retrieved December 8, 2013, from http://www.joe.org/joe/2009june/tt2.php.

Rapoport, A. (2014, March). Inside the Mind of Bobby Flay. *Bon appetit*, Vol. 59 Issue 3, 83.

Recipe Software with Unrivalled Power and Ease of Use. (n.d.). *Recipe software*.

Retrieved December 4, 2013, from http://www.livingcookbook.com.

Reinhart, P. (2001). *The bread baker's apprentice: mastering the art of extraordinary bread* (p. 90). Berkeley: Ten Speed Press.

Rodd, T., & Bryant, G. (2007). Ocimum. *The plant finder: the right plants for every garden* (p. 748). Richmond Hill, Ont.: Firefly Books.

Ruhlman, M. (2009). Stocks and the Amazing Things They Allow You to Do. *Ratio: the simple codes behind the craft of everyday cooking* (p. 92). New York, NY: Scribner.

Schnell, S. M. (2007). Food With A Farmer's Face: Community-Supported Agriculture In The United States. *Geographical review*, 97(4), 550-564.

ServSafe coursebook (5th ed., pp. 6-9). (2008). The Flow of Food: Purchasing and Receiving. Chicago, IL: National Restaurant Association Solutions.

Simonds, J. O. (1983). *Landscape architecture: a manual of site planning and design*. New York: McGraw-Hill.

Simonetti-Bryan, J. (2010). Wine for Any Occasion and Any Food. *The every-day guide to wine* (p. 115). Chantilly, VA: The Teaching Company.

Spirn, A. W. (1984). *The granite garden: urban nature and human design*. New York: Basic Books.

Stuckey, B. (2013). How the Pros Taste. *Taste: surprising stories and science about why food tastes good* (p. 33, 138). New York: Atria.

Swink, F. (1979). *Plants of the Chicago region; a check list of the vascular flora of the Chicago region with notes on local distribution and ecology,*. Lisle, Ill.: Morton Arboretum.

The State of Our Chicago Wilderness: A Report Card on the Ecological Health of the Region (p. 24). (2006). Terrestrial and Aquatic Communities. The Chicago

Wilderness consortium: Chicago Wilderness.

Totally Tomatoes. (2014). *Totally tomatoes catalog* 2014. Randolph, WI: Author.

Tucker, A. O., & DeBaggio, T. (2009). Herb Profiles. *The encyclopedia of herbs a comprehensive reference to herbs of flavor and fragrance* (2nd ed., p. 393). Portland: Timber Press.

U.S. Food and Drug Administration. (n.d.). *How to Understand and Use the Nutrition Facts Label.* Retrieved March 2, 2014, from http://www.fda.gov/food/ingredientspackaginglabeling/labelingnutrition/ucm274593.htm.

Walker, R. (2003, November 30). The Guts of a New Machine. *The new york times.* Retrieved May 13, 2014, from http://www.nytimes.com/2003/11/30/magazine/30IPOD.html

Wang, R. (n.d.). How to Make Sweet and Sour Chicken. *Art of Cooking.* Retrieved March 15, 2014, from https://www.youtube.com/watch?v=G4Qr_Eqtrc4&list=TL4Nwog7rk2bzOIm0qzr1icAhcnh20kTEJ

Weight of Water. (n.d.). *WolframAlpha knowledge engine.* Retrieved April 20, 2014, from http://www.wolframalpha.com/input/?i=1.041%09ounce+avoirdupois

Wholey, J. S., Hatry, H. P., & Newcomer, K. E. (2004). Implementation Evaluation. *Handbook of practical program evaluation* (2nd ed., pp. 66-67). San Francisco, CA: Jossey-Bass.

Williams, N. S., Thompson, K., McDonnell, M. J., Norton, B. A., Duncan, R. P., Corlett, R. T., et al. (2009). A Conceptual Framework For Predicting The Effects Of Urban Environments On Floras. *Journal of ecology,* 97(1), 4-9.

Zint, M. (n.d.). Evaluation: What is it and why do it? *My environmental education evaluation resource assistant.* Retrieved December 8, 2013, from http://meera.snre.umich.edu/plan-an-evaluation/evaluation-what-it-and-why-do-it.

REFERENCES

RECIPES

Index

A

Acidity, 52, 56, 85
Acorn Squash, 152
Agave Nectar, 22, 52
Aji-No-Moto (MSG), 53
Alcohol, 54, 57
Allspice, 63, 67,152
Almonds, 149, 153
Amaranth, 141
Amelanchier canadensis, 70
Amino Acids, 52
Anchovies, 58, 144, 147
Apple Cider, 153
Apricot, 133, 152
Aquatic Invertebrates, 71
Aroma
    evaluation, 55, 115, 117
    fixing, 57, 141
    flavor component, 50, 53-54, 139
    reheating, 57, 118
    volatiles, 54, 61
Aromatics, 9, 64, 88, 95-96
Artichoke, 133, 146, 148, 152
Artichoke Hearts, 17-18, 20
Arugula, 52, 148
As-Purchased (AP) Price, 132
Asparagus, 150, 154
Aspartame, 153
Astringency, 53, 76
Avocado, 55, 133

B

Bacon, 52, 55, 64, 140, 147, 155
Baker's Percentage, 13-15, 24
Baking, 11, 31
    See Also Cooking Methods
Baking and Pastries, 2, 11
Baking Soda, 67

Balsamic Vinegar, 37, 140

Banana, 133, 152

Banana Pepper, 136

Barbecuing, 31
    See Also Cooking Methods

Barley, 152

Bartlett Pear, 136

Basil, 51, 60, 66, 146, 152

Basting, 33

Battered Items, 31

Beans, 152

Beer, 149

Beet, 133, 146, 152

Bell Pepper, 152

Biodiversity, 71

Bitter, 50-55, 60-63, 75, 140, 148
    See Also Taste

Bitter Greens, 55

Blue Cheese, 147

Bok Choy, 133

Bones
    affect on serving size, 16
    beef, 8, 53
    brown stock, 63, 65
    chicken, 9-10
    impurities, 8, 45
    white stocks, 8-9, 43, 53, 88

Braising, 33, 84, 87
    See Also Cooking Methods

Bread
    baker's percentage, 13-14
    hydration, 15

Breading, 31

Broccoli Florets, 17-18, 20

Broiling, 29-30, 87
    See Also Cooking Methods

Broth, 3, 8

Browning, 29, 33, 52, 62, 84
    See Also Maillard Reaction

Brunoise Knife Cut, 64

Brussels Sprout, 133, 148

Buffet Dining, 2, 16, 18-19, 24

Butcher's Twine, 101

Butchering, 28

Buttermilk, 151

Butternut Squash, 152

C

Cabbage, 133, 154

Cabbage - Napa, 133

Cabernet Sauvignon, 85, 88, 95

Cajun Cuisine, 66

Camembert Cheese, 147

Canola Oil, 5-8

Cantaloupe, 133

Capers, 146

Carambola Fruit, 137

Caramelization, 33

Caraway Seeds, 65, 148

Carbohydrates, 33

Cardamom, 152

Carrot Sizes, 134

Carryover Cooking, 36

Cashew Nuts, 22

Cauliflower, 133, 148

Cayenne Pepper, 66

Celeriac Root, 134, 146

Celery
    beef pairing, 68
    browning, 102
    chicken soup, 43-44

component of *mirepoix*, 9

seed, 146

sodium content, 22, 146

weight, 134

Ceviche, 28-29

Cheddar Cheese, 56, 147, 155

Cheeseburger, 56, 139

Cherries, 150

Chervil, 146

Chestnuts, 153

Chicory, 148

Chili Pepper

Cajun cuisine, 66

piquancy, 53

sodium content, 146

Chili Powder, 146

Chinese Buffet, 16

Chinese Eggplant, 134

Chorizo, 147

Ciabatta, 14

Cilantro, 148

Cinnamon, 50, 62-64, 152

Citrus, 53

Cooking Equipment, 119

Cooking Methods, 28-33, 124

barbecuing, 31

braising, 33

broiling, 29

deep-frying, 31

grilling, 30

pan-frying, 31

poaching and boiling, 32

roasting and baking, 31

sauté, 29

simmering, 32

steaming, 32

stewing, 33

Cooking Techniques

definition, 38, 45

deglaze, 88

identification in recipes, 33

importance, 38

recipe selection, 46, 124

layering, 59-65, 77

pincer, 88

See Also Cooking Methods

Clams, 147

Clementines, 152

Cloves, 146, 152

Coconut, 134, 152

Cod, 155

Coffee, 49, 52-53, 55, 149

Cold Foods, 1

Also See Hot Foods

Collard Green, 140

Community Supported

Agriculture, 69

Conservation, 68

Consumer Recipes, 3-5, 88,

91-92, 124

See Also Home Cook

Conversion Factor, 17-20

Coriander, 60, 64, 146, 152

Corn, 134, 152, 154

Cornelian Cherry Dogwood

Cornus mas, 52

sour taste, 52, 150

Cornmeal, 146

Cornstarch, 141

Cosmi Finance, 22

Court Bouillon, 32

Crab, Alaska King, 147, 153

Cranberries, 150

Cream of Tartar, 150

Crème Fraiche, 151

Crosshatch Marks, 29-30

Cucumber, 40, 67, 134, 148, 150

Cuisine Type, 67

Cultivated Food Species, 69, 72
     75, 77

Cumin

    Middle Eastern cuisine, 62-64

    sodium content, 146

    taste profile, 50, 148

    toasting, 60

Currants, 152

D

Daikon Radish, 134

Dairy Products, 147, 151, 153

Dairy Queen, 68

Dandelion, 148

Deboning, 9

Deep-Frying, 31

    Also See Cooking Methods

Defatting, 35, 87-90

Deglazing, 35, 61, 64-65

    Also See Cooking Techniques

Denatured Protein, 28

    Also See Ceviche

Design, 81

Design Process, 82

Dill Weed, 146

Dining Context, 15, 24

Dry-Heat Cooking, 29

    See Also Cooking Methods

Dry Ounces, 9, 41, 46, 110

E

Eddoe, 137

Eggplant, 67, 148, 134

Eggs, 32

Endangered Species, 68

Enoki, 150

Enokitake, 154

Entrée Protein 15-16,

Escarole, 134, 148

Evaluation

    benefit, 114

    context, 82, 113

    formative, 115

    outcomes, 117

    process, 116

    summative, 115, 120

    quantitative, 118

Evaporation

    sauce development, 33, 35, 57,
        88, 90

    water loss, 9

F

Fabrication, 28, 91

Farmers Market, 57, 69

Farro, 22

Fast Food Restaurants, 56, 69

Fat Separator, 103, 107

Fattiness, 52, 56, 141

Fava Bean Pod, 134

Fennel, 134, 152

Feta Cheese, 147

Figs, 152

Finger Pinches, 51

Fish Sauce, 52, 58, 147, 155

Five Star Ratings, 33, 35

Flavor

    balancing, 55. 59-65

    brightening, 52, 56, 57, 65, 140

    components, 50

    development, 50

    flavor profile, 54, 55, 59, 76, 118

    layering, 59-61, 77

    pairings, 55-56

Fleur de Sel, 51

Fond, 102

Formative Evaluation, 115

Fragmented Lands, 68

French Bread, 14-15

French Vinaigrette, 4, 40

Frisée, 134, 148

Fructose, 52, 140

Fuji Apple, 133

G

Gala Apple, 55, 140

Galangal, 150

Garde Manger, 1

Garlic, 134, 148

General Tso's Chicken, 16

Ginger

    carrot ginger dressing, 41-43

    pairing, 67

    sweet and sour chicken, 38-39

    taste profile, 148

Gobo Root - Japan, 134

Gobo Root - Taiwan, 134

Gorgonzola Cheese, 147

Gouda Cheese, 147

Graduated Glassware, 11-12

Grains, 12, 144, 146-154

Granny Smith Apple, 63, 65, 133

    150

Grape Hyacinths, 70

Grapefruit, 52, 135, 140, 150, 154

Grape, 52, 140, 150, 154

Gremolata, 34, 140

Grilling, 30, 56, 67, 155

    See Also Cooking Methods

Groundwater, 71

Guava, 152

H

Habanero Pepper, 136

Habitat Types

    boggy, 75

    prairie, 68

    wetland, 68

    woodland, 68, 71, 72, 115

Ham, 140, 147, 155

Hawaiian Red Salt, 51

Hazelnuts, 73, 153

Heat Conduction, 30

Heirloom Vegetables, 57, 68

Himalayan Salt, 51

Hoisin Sauce, 143, 147, 153

Home Cook, 2-4, 7, 9, 23, 27, 33

    92, 98

    See Also Consumer Recipes

Honey, 42, 52-53, 59, 141, 153

Honey Crisp Apple, 133

Honeydew Melon, 135

Horticultural Methods, 69

Hosui Pear, 136

Hot Foods
    cooking methods, 28
    definition, 1
    flavor layering, 60
    piquancy, 53, 67
    ratios, 11
Hygroscopic Sugars, 59

I

Ichiban Eggplant, 134
Ingredient
    quantities, 3, 7, 57, 84
    relationships, 57, 116, 124-125
    substitution, 59, 60-61, 76
Invertebrate, 71
Italian Salad Dressing, 17-18, 20

J

Jalapeno Pepper, 21-22, 136
Japan, 53, 66-67, 134
Japanese Tempura, 32
Jennings Digital Scale, 12
Jicama, 135, 152
Juneberry, 70, 152
Juneberry Jam, 12

K

Kabocha Squash, 135, 152
Kaffir Lime, 150
Kaki Japanese Persimmon, 136
Kale, 148
Katsuobushi, 155
Kelp, 146, 154

Ketchup, 39, 52, 155
Kikkoman Soy Sauce, 58
Kiwi Fruit, 135, 150
Knife Skills, 38
Kombu, 154
Kool-Aid, 67
Kumquats, 150

L

Ladle, 8, 89, 103, 107-108
Landscape Architecture, 82, 109
Leek, 132, 135, 150
Lemon, 52-53, 56, 135, 140-141, 146
    148, 150
Lemon Juice
    brightening flavor, 52, 140
    ceviche, 28
Lemongrass, 135, 150
Lentils, 61-65
Lettuce, Iceberg, 135
Lettuce, Romaine, 148
Lima Beans, 148
Lime, 53, 56, 135, 150
Lobster, 140, 153, 155
Lotus Root, 135, 152

M

Mace, 146
MacGourmet Software, 22
Mackerel, 147, 155
Madagascar Bourbon, 57
Maillard Reaction, 33
    See Also Browning
Marjoram, 130, 146, 152

Malt Vinegar, 140

Mango, 135, 152

Marinara Sauce, 59-60

Marinating, 84

Marshmallows, 59-60

Mary Mix McDonald Woods, 71

MasterCook Software, 22

Melons, 152

Middle Eastern Cuisine, 66

Ming Tsai, 66

Mint, 66, 152

Mirepoix, 9-10, 44, 64, 88-92

Mirin, 153

Mise en Place, 104

Miso, 147, 151, 155

Moist-Heat Cooking, 29, 32-33,
    34-35, 44, 84-87, 103-104
    See Also Cooking Methods

Molasses, 153

Monosodium Glutamate, 53, 61

Moroccan Cuisine, 50

Mouthfeel, 53, 56-57, 76, 91, 104
    See Also Flavor

Museum Exhibits, 114-115

Mushroom, 52, 63, 68, 135, 150,
    154

Mussels, 153

Mustard, 148

Mustard Sauce, 141

N

Napa Cabbage, 133

Nappe, 88, 91, 108

Natural Areas Preservation, 71

Navel Oranges, 21, 135

Nectarines, 152

Negi (Japanese Onion), 135

New Zealand Spinach, 146

Nutmeg, 152

Nutrition
    food values, 20,22, 24
    meal planning, 5
    USDA database, 22

O

Oil Backsplash, 31

Olive Oil
    pairing, 67
    salad dressings, 7-8

Olives, 146

Onion
    caramelizing, 37, 62-64
    sweet taste, 152
    umami taste, 154
    weight, 135

Oregano
    Origanum majoricum, 130
    Origanum onites, 130
    Origanum vulgare, 130
    Origanum vulgare subsp. hirtum,
        130
    sprig, 135
    taste profile, 148

Original Yield, 17-19

Ornamental Tree, 70

Oyster Sauce, 147

Oysters, 155

P

Pairing, 50, 55-56, 66-68, 76-77,

124, 139-141

See Also Flavor

Pan Overloading, 29, 101-102

Pancakes, 141

Pancetta, 147

Papaya, 152

Paprika, 152

Parasites, 29

Paring Knife, 103

Parmesan Cheese

    sodium content, 147

    taste profile, 155

    umami pairing, 52, 141, 155

Parsley

    dried taste profile, 146, 152

    flat-leaved weight, 135

    garnish, 130

    Petroselinum crispum, 130

    Petroselinum crispum

        neapolitanum, 130

    salt content, 146

    stem weight, 136

Parsnip, 136, 152

Passion Fruit, 152

Pasta, 16, 19, 140

Pasteurized, 147

Peaches, 152

Pears, 52, 152

Peas

    pairing, 66

    side dish, 16

    taste profile, 152, 154

Pecorino Cheese, 147

Peppers

    chili, 53

    roasted red, 59

pineapple chicken, 38

Persimmon

    kaki, 136

    taste profile, 152

    weight,136

Photographic Images, 99

Pickled Plums, 66

Pickles, 146, 150

Pie Dough

    3-2-1 basic, 11

Pimentos, 152

Pincer, 88, 90

    See Also Cooking Techniques

Pineapple

    chicken, 38

    taste profile, 152

    weight, 136

Piquancy, 53, 67, 141

    See Also Flavor

Plant Communities

    description, 69

    flatwoods, 71-73

Plantains, 152

Poach, 32, 35-36

    See Also Cooking Methods

Pomegranate

    taste profile, 150

    weight,136

Ponzu, 151

Poppy Seeds, 152

Pork, 155

Portion Size

    professional recipes, 6

    recipe interpretation, 124

    restaurants, 16, 24

Potatoes, 117, 134, 140, 152

Prairie, 68, 73
  See Also Habitats
Prawns, 155
Preserved Lemons, 146
Professional Kitchen, 1, 4
Professional Recipes, 2, 4-6, 23,
  28, 34, 46, 124
Professional Tasters, 118
Prosciutto, 147
Provolone Cheese, 147
Prunes, 152
Prunus mume, 66
Pumpkin, 152

Q

Qualitative Methods, 118, 120
Quantitative Methods, 115, 118
Quince, 150

R

Radicchio, 148
Radish, 55, 139-140, 148
Raisins, 152
Ratios, 2, 7, 9, 11-12, 24, 43
Ready-to-Eat Foods, 69
Recipes
  basic chicken stock, 10
  basic French bread, 14
  basic French dressing, 6, 8
  braised saffron chicken and
    leeks, 35
  braised short ribs in red wine
    sauce, 85, 86, 94
  citrus salsa, 21

classic chicken soup, 43-44
Italian tri-colored rotini salad,
  17-18, 20
Japanese carrot ginger salad
  dressing, 41-42
lemon poached shrimp, 35-36
Middle Eastern lentils in wine
  sauce, 63
oven braised short ribs, 88-92
  94, 96, 100, 106
sautéed pork chops with
  balsamic onions, 37
seasoned lentils, 61
seasoned Middle Eastern
  lentils, 62
sweet and sour chicken, 39
Recipe Concepts, 84-85
Recipe Documentation, 117, 125
Recipe Errors, 2, 12, 28, 56, 84
Recipe Interpretation, 27, 44-45,
  123-126
Recipe Layout
  balance, 99
  chunking, 98
  consistency, 98
  ingredient list, 99
  pictures, 99, 104-109
  repetition, 98
  symmetry, 99
  text, 98-99
  white space, 99
Recipe Readability, 98-99
Recipe Yield
  changing, 15-20
Red Ancient Sweet Pepper, 136
Red Potato, 136

Reduction
    description, 35
    flavor enhancement, 108, 118
    sauce making, 88, 90, 104, 141
    sauce texture, 141
Regional Cuisine, 66
Rhubarb, 52, 136, 150
Risotto, 140
Roasting, 31
    See Also Cooking Methods
Roma Tomato, 21, 137
Romano Cheese, 147
Roquefort Cheese, 136
Rosemary
    flavor profile, 148
    Rosarinus officinalis, 130
    sprig size, 132, 136
    sprig weight, 136
Roux, 57, 104, 118
Russet Potato, 136
Rutabaga, 136

S

S'more, 59-60
Saccharine, 153
Sachet, 9, 88, 90, 101
Saffron, 146, 148
Sage, 52, 141, 148
Sake, 153
Salami, 147
Saltiness
    description, 50-51, 75
    fixing, 55, 140-141
    pairing, 56, 140
    ingredients, 58, 146-147

Sardines, 155
Satoimo, 136
Sautéing, 29
    See Also Cooking Methods
Savory
    umami taste, 52, 54, 76
Scaling
    description, 5, 23, 46
    digital, 12, 41, 46
    vegetables, 40, 129, 133
Scallop, 153, 155
Searing, 28, 38
Seasonal Woodland Pond, 71
Seasonings, 6
Seaweed, 52, 146
Serving Size
    professional recipes, 4-5
    recipe yields, 15-24
Sesame Seed, 152
Shallot, 136
Shaoxing Wine, 39
Sherry Wine, 63, 153
Shiraz Wine, 88
Shitake Mushroom, 154
Shrimp, 28, 32, 35, 36, 153
Silverskin, 89, 91, 100, 105
Simmering
    chicken soup, 44-45
    definition, 32
    lentils, 61-62
    short ribs, 87
    white stock, 53
    See Also Cooking Methods
Skimming, 44-45
    See Also Cooking Techniques
Slurry, 57, 141

Small Dice, 40

Smartphone, 54, 117

Smell, 49-50, 53-54, 75-76
> *See Also* Aroma

Sodium Chloride, 51, 53

Software, 22, 24, 125

Sourness
> component of taste, 51-52
> offset by, 55-56, 141
> pairs with, 140-141
> *See Also* Taste

Soy Sauce, 58-59, 147, 151, 155

Soybean Paste, 42, 58

Spearmint, 146

Spices,
> layering, 60, 64
> piquancy, 67, 141, 153
> taste profile, 146-155

Spinach, 146, 148

Sprig
> description, 129-132
> oregano, 130-131, 135
> parsley, 13-131, 135
> rosemary, 130, 132, 136
> thyme, 130, 137

Squash Acorn, 152, 136

Squid, 155

Standardized Recipe
> adapting for home, 23
> creating, 98
> purpose, 4

Star Fruit, 137

Starches, 16, 19, 24, 140

Steaming, 32, 61
> *See Also* Cooking Methods

Steve Jobs, 81

Stevia, 153

Stewing, 33
> *See Also* Cooking Methods

Stocks
> cloudy, 8
> development, 8
> impurities, 8, 10, 45
> white stocks, 8-9, 43, 53, 88-89

Strawberries, 56, 72,140, 152

Sucralose, 153

Sucrose, 52

Sumac, 150

Summative Evaluation, 115, 120

Summer Squash, 136

Sweating, 29-30, 34-35, 65
> *See Also* Cooking Techniques

Sweeteners
> balanced by, 140-141
> hygroscopic nature, 59
> natural, 52
> taste profile, 147-155

Swimming method, 31-32
> *See Also* Deep-Frying

Swiss Chard, 146

Swiss Cheese, 147

Syrah Wine, 88

T

Tabasco Sauce, 67

Tabbouleh, 130

Tamarind, 150

Tangerine, 137, 152

Tannins in Wine, 53-54

Taro, 137

Tarragon, 148, 150

Taste
    adjusting, 55-56
    components, 50-52
    ingredient substitutions, 60-61
Texture
    chewy, 91
    fixing sauces, 141
    flavor relationship, 49-50, 53,
        76-77, 91, 115
    mouthfeel, 53-54
    sauces, 65
    visual appearance in nature, 73
Thickeners, 141
Thyme
    sodium content, 51
    sprig, 137
    taste profile, 148
    Thymus vulgaris, 130
Tomatillo, 137
Tomatoes
    pairs with, 140-141
    taste profile, 150
    transportability, 57
    umami taste, 56-154
    weight, 137
Truffles, 154
Tuna, 155
Turkey Gravy, 58-59
Turmeric, 52, 148
Turnip, 137, 148
Tzatziki Sauce, 56

U

Umami
    Aji-no-moto, 53
    component of taste, 51-52, 75-76
    description, 52
    mushrooms, 154
    pairing with, 55, 141
    taste table, 154
    turkey gravy, 58
    white stock, 53
    See Also Taste
Umeboshi, 66
Undertones, 60
    See Also Flavor

V

Vanilla, 57, 68, 153
Vermouth, 153
Vidalia Onion, 55
Vinaigrette, 4-5, 7, 40, 140
Volatiles, 54, 61
    See Also Aroma
Volume Measures
    definition, 5
    problems encountered, 42-43
    working with, 7, 11-12
    See Also Scaling

W

Wakame, 146, 154
Walnuts, 155, 149
Watercress, 55, 139-140, 148
Watermelon, 152
Websites
    America's Test Kitchen, 3
    Epicurious, 3
    recipe searching, 85

The Fresh Loaf, 3
Wheat, 152
Whey, 151
Whisk, 38-39
White Wine, 35, 63, 65
Wok, 29, 39
Woodland Canopy, 73
Woodland Communities, 71
    See Also Habitat Types
Woodland Species
    American hazelnut
        Corylus americana, 73
    black-eyed Susan,
        Rudbeckia hirta, 75
    Canada blue grass
        Poa compressa, 75
    colic root
        Aletris farinosa, 75
    common boneset
        Eupatorium perfoliatum, 75
    common cinquefoil
        Potentilla simplex, 75
    enchanter's nightshade
        *Circaea quadrisulcata
            canadensis*, 73
    false toadflax
        Comandra richardsiana, 73
    horsetail
        Equisetum arvense, 73
    mash shield fern
        *Dryopteris thelypteris
            pubescens*, 75
    orange jewelweed
        Impatiens capensis, 72, 73
    prairie phlox
        Phlox pilosa, 75
    royal fern
        *Osmunda regalis
            spectablilis*, 75
    sky-blue aster
        Aster azureus, 73
    swamp white oak
        Quercus bicolor, 73
    tall goldenrod
        Solidago altissima, 73
    wild geranium
        Geranium maculatum, 72-73
    wild onion
        Allium canadense, 73
    wild strawberry
        Fragaria virginiana, 71-73
    woodland brome
        Bromus pubescens, 73
    yarrow
        Achillea millefolium, 75
Woodland Understory, 73
Worcestershire Sauce, 155

Y

Yam, 137, 152
Yogurt, 56, 140, 151
Yucca Root, 137
Yuzu Fruit, 150

Z

Zinfandel Wine, 88
Zucchini, 137, 148

Made in the USA
Charleston, SC
12 December 2014